QUODVULTDEUS OF CARTHAGE

The Creedal Homilies

Ancient Christian Writers

THE WORKS OF THE FATHERS IN TRANSLATION

MANAGING EDITOR
Dennis D. McManus

EDITORIAL BOARD
Walter J. Burghardt
John Dillon

No. 60

QUODVULTDEUS OF CARTHAGE: THE CREEDAL HOMILIES

Conversion in Fifth-Century North Africa

TRANSLATION AND COMMENTARY

BY

THOMAS MACY FINN

THE NEWMAN PRESS
New York/Mahwah, N.J.

Jacket design by Cynthia Dunne

Library of Congress Cataloging-in-Publication Data

Quodvultdeus, Bishop of Carthage, d. 454?
   [De symbolo. 1-3. English]
   Quodvultdeus of Carthage : the creedal homilies : conversion in fifth-century North Africa / translation and commentary by Thomas Macy Finn.
      p. cm.—(Ancient Christian writers; no. 60)
   ISBN 0-8091-0572-1 (alk. paper)
   1. Nicene Creed—Sermons. 2. Conversion—Christianity—Sermons. 3. Sermons, Latin—Translations into English. I. Finn, Thomas M. (Thomas Macy), 1927–. II. Title. III. Series.
   BR60.A35 no. 60
   [BR65.Q663]
   270s—dc22
   [252/.014]

                                                              2004003008

Published by The Newman Press
an imprint of Paulist Press
997 Macarthur Boulevard
Mahwah, New Jersey 07430

www.paulistpress.com

PRINTED AND BOUND IN THE UNITED STATES OF AMERICA

CONTENTS

ABBREVIATIONS

ACW   Ancient Christian Writers. New York: Newman/Paulist, 1946–.

ANF   Ante-Nicene Fathers. Edited by A. Roberts and J. Donaldson. Reprint. Peabody: Hendrickson, 1994.

ATAE   *Augustine Through the Ages: An Encyclopedia.* Edited by Allan D. Fitzgerald et al. Grand Rapids/Cambridge: William B. Eerdmans, 1999.

CCL   Corpus Christianorum, series Latina. Turnhout: Brepols, 1953–.

CSEL   Corpus scriptorum ecclesiasticorum latinorum. Vienna: Gerodi, 1866–.

CSCO   Corpus scriptorum christianorum orientalium. Paris: Reipublicae; Leipzig: Harrassowitz; Louvain: Peeters, 1902–.

DS   *Dictionnaire de la spiritualité.* Edited by M. Villers et al. Paris: Beauchesne, 1970–.

DTC   *Dictionnaire de théolgie catholique.* Edited by A. Vacant et al. Paris: Letouzey et Ané, 1903–1950.

EEC   *Encyclopedia of Early Christianity.* Edited by E. Ferguson. 2nd ed. New York: Garland, 1997.

ELA   *Ephemerides Liturgicae Analecta.* Louvain, 1924–.

ER   *Encyclopedia of Religion.* Edited by Mircea Eliade. New York: Macmillan, 1987.

FC   Fathers of the Church. Washington: Catholic University of America Press, 1947–.

HDS   Harvard Dissertation Series

HTR   *Harvard Theological Review*

JAAR   *Journal of the American Academy of Religion*

JBL	*Journal of Biblical Literature*
JEC	*Journal of Early Christian Studies*
JTS	*Journal of Theological Studies*
MF	Message of the Fathers of the Church. Edited by Thomas Halton. Collegeville, MN: Liturgical Press (Michael Glazier Books), 1987–.
PL	*Patrologia Latina*. Paris, 1844–64.
REAug	*Revue des études augustiniennes*
RHE	*Revue d'Histroire Ecclésiastique*
SC	Sources Chrétiennes. Paris: Éditions du Cerf, 1941–.
SCA	Studies in Christian Antiquity. Edited by Johannes Quasten. Washington: Catholic University Press, 1941–.
SST	Studies in Sacred Theology. Washington: Catholic University of America Press.
Theotokos	*Theotokos: A Theological Encyclopedia of the Blessed Virgin Mary*. Edited by Michael O'Carroll. Collegeville, MN: Liturgical Press, 1990.
VC	*Vigiliae Christianae: A Review of Early Christian Life and Language*

PREFACE

The history of scholarship, it is said, is the history of scholars. Every book, it may be added, has a personal history—at least this one has. My teaching life has been devoted to the worlds of early and medieval Christianity. My scholarly life has been devoted to what turns out to be the wellspring of those worlds, the rites of Christian worship, in particular, the early Christian liturgy of initiation. At the heart of my interest is, and has been, conversion and how it was enacted in rite and symbol. At the outset of my career, my interest was inspired and shaped by the late Reverend Doctor Johannes Quasten, the world-renowned patrologist and professor of Christian history and archaeology at the Catholic University of America. He set me to work on the newly discovered baptismal instructions of John Chrysostom, the results of which were published in the university's Studies in Christian Antiquity, which he edited.

In many ways, I have been writing that first book ever since, although my interests have expanded from west Syria to the Syrian east, Italy, Egypt, and North Africa. As I pursued my interests in the early Christian ritual world, I discovered two curiously and fortunately related facts. In the academic world, several decades ago ritual was hidden away in a closet labeled, "Beware: Superstition." Historians of liturgy and symbolic anthropologists, however, opened that closet door to show an increasingly interested world inside and outside the academy how the study of the ritual process opens onto the cultural world of the needs, crises, expectations, and fundamental values of societies ancient and modern. Without the work of liturgical historians and symbolic anthropologists I would have been unable to explore the dynamics of conversion in Christian, Jewish, and pagan antiquity, and depict the situation and experience of Christians, Jews, and pagans in the process of transformation.

So it was no surprise, at least to me, that the recently recovered baptismal homilies on the creed of Quodvultdeus, the last pre-Vandal bishop of Carthage, captured my interest. I am deeply grate-

ix

ful that Paulist Press's distinguished Ancient Christian Writers series matched my interest in publishing this first English translation of his homilies and commentary. The work was made possible by two institutions and furthered by many people. The institution that gave focus to my interest in Quodvultdeus is the National Council on U.S.–Arab Relations. In 1992, the council awarded me a summer fellowship in Tunisia that permitted me to explore the remains of ancient Carthage and the other striking Roman sites in the country, making it possible for me to meet Emily Williams, Associate Archeological Conservator for the Colonial Williamsburg Foundation, who gave me a thorough on-site initiation into the excavations at Carthage's circus. The institution that has given my research practical encouragement and support is the College of William and Mary, with its policy of summer research grants and extended research assignments. To further my work on Quodvultdeus the College awarded me a grant that enabled me to devote the summer of 1995 to the homilies, followed by a research assignment covering the academic year 1996–1997.

Among the people to whom I am deeply indebted are the Reverend Michael W. Heintz, of the School of Theology at the University of Notre Dame, who provided me with unpublished manuscripts of his translations of Quodvultdeus's first and second creedal homilies and the bishop's homilies *De cantico novo* and *Adversus quinque haereses;* and Dr. Dennis D. McManus, managing editor of Ancient Christian Writers, who provided me consistently with encouragement and insight for my translation and commentary—especially valuable because of his rich and ready classical and patristic background. Closer to home is my wife, Marielena Vidrio Finn, who regularly lent me her expertise as a systems analyst; and Tamara A. Cooper, of the College's Department of Religion, who was always at hand to resolve word-processing enigmas and to prepare a readable manuscript for the editors.

Thomas M. Finn
Chancellor Professor of Religion, Emeritus
College of William and Mary
Williamsburg, Virginia
September 2003

INTRODUCTION

Quodvultdeus

"Beloved Son and Fellow Deacon"—an aged Augustine's greeting to his young colleague Deacon Quodvultdeus of Carthage, the author of the creedal homilies. The two corresponded in 428–429, the deacon importuning the bishop to compose a handbook of heresies for the clergy of Carthage. After putting him off several times, Augustine composed *De haeresibus ad Quodvultdeum*, cataloguing eighty-eight heresies, beginning with the Simonian Gnostics and ending with the Pelagians.[1]

Quodvultdeus was known also to the historian of the Vandal invasion, Victor of Vita, not as deacon but as bishop of Carthage. In fact, Victor reports that the Vandal king Geiseric, who took Carthage in 439, banished the bishop and a throng of his clergy, incarcerating them naked on leaky ships ostensibly to drown. He adds, however, that with God as navigator the bishop's sinking ship made it to Naples.[2]

In plain hard fact, that is all we know about Quodvultdeus, deacon and bishop. Much more might be added, if one forages in the works now generally assigned to him.[3] But there is no slight problem. Until 1914, when Dom G. Morin first identified Quodvultdeus as author of a dozen homiletic works, Quodvultdeus was "Pseudo-Augustine."[4] Among the homilies rescued from pseudo-Augustinian status were five delivered to catechumens soon to be baptized, plus seven more for a wider audience. A thirteenth work—his longest, most unusual, and most influential—is the *Liber promissionum*, for centuries attributed to Prosper of Aquitaine (c. 390–c. 486) in recognition of its importance and subsequent influence. Indeed, by the tenth century it was considered a normative work for biblical interpretation.[5] Composed of biblical *testimonia* arranged according to Augustine's tripartite division of salvation history—before the law *(ante legem)*, under the law *(sub lege)*, and under grace *(sub gratia,* divided between

1

the signs of the Antichrist and the glory and reign of the saints)[6]—the *Liber* sought to underscore what Quodvultdeus saw as the christological, ecclesiastical, and apocalyptic thrust of the Bible. Following the lead of Morin and others, Réné Braun first attempted to establish Quodvultdeus as the author of the *Liber,* and then of twelve homiletic works ascribed to others, including Augustine. The now-exiled bishop wrote the *Liber* in the evening of his life in Naples.[7]

If one accepts the twelve homilies as works of the Carthaginian bishop—and not every one does[8]—a fuller vita is possible. Quodvultdeus was born in Carthage about 390 and was given a typically Latinized Punic theonym, "what God wills." His homilies bespeak a man of sound rhetorical education—the kind one might expect in the Carthage Augustine knew—but they also indicate a young man who early headed for a religious life of service to the church. We find him a deacon of the church at Carthage under Bishop Aurelius (c. 390–c. 430) about 420, a highly visible and important post that he held until he became assistant bishop to the successor of Aurelius, Capreolus (c. 435). In turn, he succeeded Capreolus about 437. In his creedal homilies, preached in the 430s, one hears the agony of a city beset by internal religious division as it must gradually face the brutalities of Geiseric and the Vandals, to which it eventually falls. The *Liber,* which the editor dates about 450, suggests that he participated actively in the life of the church at Naples, all the while longing for his native city. His see at Carthage remained vacant until 457, when Deogratias was consecrated, indicating that by then Quodvultdeus had died in Naples.

Perhaps more could be added to the vita of Quodvultdeus, but detailed studies of his work are at an early stage. Nonetheless, two general observations are both supportable and relevant. First, he was deeply indebted to Augustine in the approach, content, hermeneutics, and rhetoric of his extant works. It is no accident that for centuries his works were considered Pseudo-Augustinian. But Quodvultdeus was the pastoral leader of the church in proconsular Africa, not, like Augustine, the church's intellectual leader. Thus, in his works one can begin to gauge the distinctive pastoral influence of Augustine on his North African colleagues, especially in catechesis, doctrine, and hermeneutics.

Second, one finds aggressive, even vituperative, polemic in Quodvultdeus's works against Jews, pagans, and heretics. Granted that late antiquity was a world habituated to the classical rhetoric of degradation, the timbre of his vituperation is also an indication of a church besieged both within and without. Pagans were far from recumbent, the Jews hardly abject, and the heretics not a bit daunted. And then, of course, there are the Vandals, who, eighty thousand strong with Geiseric at their head (438–477), crossed Gibraltar's Straits in 429. They razed Hippo in 430, won most of Numidia by treaty in 435, and in 438 moved farther east to menace and, in 439, to conquer Carthage and subjugate its people, especially the city's non-Arian Christians. Echoing in Quodvultdeus's homilies, especially in *De tempore barbarico* 1 and in the ears of his audience, were those ancient words of the first Cato: *Delenda est Carthago.*[9]

THE CREEDAL HOMILIES AND THE CATECHUMENATE

The Homilies

The subject at hand, however, is the three creedal homilies now convincingly assigned to Quodvultdeus, *De symbolo* 1, 2, and 3. For centuries they were assigned to Augustine, which is where they can be found in Migne's *Patrologia Latina* (40.337–68). The text followed for translation in this volume, however, is the critical edition published by R. Braun in volume 60 of the *Corpus Christianorum, series Latina* in 1976. To assign a precise date to the homilies is hazardous, save to say that *De symbolo* 2 seems to have been first in chronological order, followed by *De symbolo* 1 and 3.[10] Since *De symbolo* 1 appears to have been delivered in the presence of Bishop Capreolus, whom Quodvultdeus succeeded in 437, all three would have been delivered in the mid-thirties of the fifth century, shortly before Quodvultdeus became bishop and the Vandals came to be a visible threat.

The creedal homilies were delivered on Sunday morning a week before Easter—perhaps before three successive Easters in the mid-430s. The setting of all three was a pivotal set of initiation rites enacted during the vigil the night before (Saturday): scrutiny, renunciation of Satan, and the profession of the baptismal creed. The target audience was those about to be baptized, the *competentes,* those who were seeking baptism together. Since they were the pivotal rites of the Lenten catechumenate, perhaps a brief description

of the catechumenate in fifth-century North Africa will provide the
context of the homilies.

The Catechumenate

The term *catechumenus* described a person inscribed in the
Latin church's register who had begun the journey to baptismal conversion.[11] The rite, inscription, that marked the formal statement of
intention to be baptized and accepted by the church involved exorcism, the imposition of hands, and the sign of the cross, coupled with
the ingestion of salt.[12] The subject could be an infant, as in
Augustine's case; an adult, as in the case of his father; or a teenager,
as in the case of Augustine's son, Adeodatus.[13] Once inscribed, they
became members of the church. As such they were the subjects of
gradual initiation into the Christian community primarily by forma-
tion in the meaning of the scriptures and the reformation of conduct.
Such was the "catechumenate," which stretched from inscription to
baptism and could encompass a lifetime. For Augustine it covered
thirty-three years, a time lapse fairly typical of the fourth and fifth
centuries, when adult baptism was the norm. Although we have no
firsthand account of why someone sought the catechumenate and
baptism apart from Augustine's in his *Confessions,* it is not possible to
assign personal motives. Given the establishment of Christianity,
from a social perspective—be it marriage, or social or economic
standing—it was better to be a Christian than not. And from a psychological perspective, the vast changes and dislocations in the
empire, unleashed by the Constantinian settlement, created in the
subjects of Rome some deep spiritual hungers that initiated quests
for a secure and nourishing source of meaning. Whatever the moti-
vation, almost in spite of it, the non-negotiable goal of the catechumenate was that personal transformation known in Latin antiquity as
conversio, and from beginning to end its setting was liturgical.[14]

An important part of the setting was oral instruction of a distinctive kind, *catechesis,* the form of which was generally a homily
centered on scripture and delivered in a liturgical setting, most often
that part of the Eucharist known in North Africa as "Mass of the
Catechumens." Indeed, the major homilists of the fourth and fifth
century saw their instructions in a sacramental light. John
Chrysostom (d. 404), for instance, viewed his baptismal catecheses

as eucharistic nourishment, frequently calling them a table laden with rich spiritual food and drink; Quodvultdeus, who saw the entire catechumenate—leading from conception in the womb of Mother Church to baptismal rebirth—speaks of his homilies as feeding "those whom she carries in her womb with proper food."[15] Nonetheless, the point was transformation enacted in slow stages. From the catechetical point of view, Quodvultdeus's creedal homilies presume the early stages, whereas Augustine develops them in his *De catechizandis rudibus*.[16] Candidates at the level of simple inquiry were called *accedentes,* because they were approaching inscription as catechumens. Once inscribed, they were "hearers" *(audientes/auditores)*. Indeed, they might remain hearers until death beckoned, as with Augustine's father, Patricius, but this practice was widely condemned by catechists and homilists at the time. But assuming that at some decisive point a hearer determined to become a baptized Christian, he or she "gave in [her or his] name" *(dat/dare nomen)* to the bishop at the start of Lent—Epiphany—for baptism at Easter. Those catechumens approved, moved from the status of *audientes* to *competentes*—they were now seeking baptism together *(petentes simul),* as Augustine puts it.[17]

Decisions not lightly made, however, are not lightly accomplished. As competents they would attend daily instruction at the Mass of the Catechumens and observe Lent rigorously: no wine, no meat, no bath, no public entertainment (Quodvultdeus uses their traditional name, *spectacula*),[18] and no marital relations. The purpose, according to Augustine, was to grind the competents as grain into flour for making that bread he calls the *corpus mysticum Christi* and thinks of as both church and Eucharist.[19]

TRADITIO SYMBOLI

Aside from enrollment for Easter baptism, the first special event was the liturgy of "the giving of the creed" *(traditio symboli)*. Celebrated in vigil on Saturday two weeks before Easter, it was a critical moment, for, as we learn from Augustine, the creed was called *symbolum,* that is, an ancient commercial contract, the terms of which spell out mutual obligations. The articles of the creed were the terms of the competents' "pact of fidelity."[20] The bishop handed over the creed, article by article, explaining each article in a few words and then calling for them to recite it together.[21] From an extant homily of Augustine on the occasion of the *traditio,* the text of the North African creed is as follows:

> I believe in God, the Father omnipotent, creator of all things, and in his Son, our Lord Jesus Christ, who was conceived of the Holy Spirit, born from the virgin, Mary. He was crucified, died, and was buried under Pontius Pilate. But on the third day he rose from the dead, ascended into heaven, sits at the right hand of God the Father, from which he will come to judge the living and the dead. And [I believe] in the Holy Spirit, the forgiveness of sins, and eternal life through the holy catholic church.[22]

In Quodvultdeus's creedal homilies these articles can be substantially verified, but the task of doing so is made difficult because his homilies are commentaries on the creed after it had been professed, rather than, as in Augustine's homily, while it was being handed over to the competents. The following week saw them, with the help of sponsors, family, and friends trying to understand and memorize the terms of their pact, for they had formally to profess it as their own the following Saturday night, again in vigil, in a rite called *redditio symboli.*

THE PIVOTAL RITES

This brings us to that night in Carthage. The congregation assembled in the church just after lamp-lighting *(lucernarium),* which signaled the arrival of evening. The competents were hidden in the shadows. Although we know some of the circumstances from Ambrose and Augustine, only Quodvultdeus is explicit about details of the vigil's first rite. Each competent was presented to the congregation: head bowed, dressed in a goatskin tunic, and barefoot on goatskin, while Psalm 138 was chanted—"Probe me, Lord, and know my heart...."[23] Although the competents had already experienced exorcisms, this rite was a solemn and sometimes shattering experience, one in which the exorcist invoked the power of Christ and the Trinity and barked biblical rebukes at the devil within. The striking

finale was "exsufflation": the exorcist grabbed hold of each competent, hissed in her or his face—the kind of action that, if done to an
imperial statue, would have brought immediate arrest for *lèse-majesté*.
In their goatskin tunics and humiliation, the competents enacted the
status of slaves bent low under servitude—and this whether they were
high-born masters or dirt-poor slaves.[24] This first rite was called
"scrutiny," because, among other things, it involved a physical exam
to see whether competents displayed any physical symptoms that
might signal continued diabolic possession, perhaps leprosy, venereal disease, or some other scabrous condition.

Next followed one of the most ancient of the prebaptismal
rites, the renunciation of Satan, his pomps, and his service. The
competents were now ready to flee the diabolic master. The exorcismal scrutiny had put the "Slave-Holder" (one of Quodvultdeus's
many epithets for Satan) to flight. Now at last each competent could
stand upright on her or his own two feet and, in perhaps quaking
voice, formally and publicly renounce that ancient slave-holder's
pomps and service.

The ancients, including Christians, shared a religious topogra-
phy in which the heavens moved in harmony—they were a cosmos—
whereas the earth tottered just above, and on the edge of, chaos, the
abode of the demonic. Earth and its inhabitants were the subjects of
demonic forces that caused every evil, small and large, including disease, death, natural cataclysms, wars, and violence.

The renunciation was a critical moment of defiance, and
Quodvultdeus leaves no doubt about what was entailed: renunciation of the pomps and service of Satan. For him, Satan's pomps and
service meant, above all, those Roman monuments to violence, illicit
pleasure, and ambition—the *spectacula:* chariot racing at the vast circus, the mimes and pantomimes in the city's celebrated theater, and
the wild animal hunts in its great amphitheater. The pomps and
service of the *new* Master, as Quodvultdeus shows with imagination
and vigor, would be quite different and would be enacted in very different arenas: spectacular miracles in the gospels, the remarkable
Esau-Jacob drama of birth, an all-powerful Daniel in the amphitheater of lion's den.[25]

With renunciation, the old *symbolum* was now null and void.
"The traps have been broken and we have been snatched away: our
help is in the name of the Lord"—so ran the words of the Psalm 123

chanted perhaps again as the finale of the rite.[26] Thus freed, the competents were now emboldened to make a new pact, the terms of which were the articles of the Carthaginian baptismal creed given them the week before at the *traditio symboli*. Whether they made the profession individually, as in Rome, or professed orally as a group is unclear.[27] In any case, the competents were empowered to do so because the evil spirit, now exorcised, had begun to give way to a new spirit, the Holy Spirit.

These three rites of the vigil were pivotal, because the ritual of conversion in North Africa turned on them as on an axis. They recapitulated for the competents their experience of an all-but-overwhelming struggle, stabilizing their determination to continue. Only one ancient autobiographical record of that struggle is extant, and that, the celebrated account of Augustine's experience in the garden at Milan.[28] The difficulty about Augustine's account is that it is read and commented on as his conversion. To be sure, he speaks of it as *conversio*, but it should be understood as the decisive moment in a process that began with his inscription as an infant thirty-three years earlier.[29] The one element he lacked previously was stability solidified by determination. The fruit he found in the Milanese garden was that stability which he had long sought. It was the gift of the catechumenate soon to be enacted in these three pivotal rites.

THE AUDIENCE

Quodvultdeus's intended audience is the competents, who had been in-course for some five weeks. Each day they had been the focus of extended instruction and frequent, perhaps daily, exorcisms, the vigor of which was designed to induce in them fear of and aversion to what they had been and, to some extent, still were. Up to this point in their journey they were "nobodies"—rather, just bodies. In a traditional figure dramatized by the pivotal rites, Quodvultdeus underscores their status as faceless slaves of Satan; every other status had been torn from them. Were some rich and of high status or poor and of no account? Were some masters and others slaves? Some of both stood in that darkened and somber church, yet all were treated the same: "Here the poor are not treated one way," we read, "the rich another, the master one way, the slave another."[30] In addition, all were dirty: no bath since Epiphany. All were hungry and thirsty: no wine, no meat, and no sex since their names were handed in. And no entertainment: no circus, no theater, no boxing, no hunt. Were any one to ask them, "Is the old self dying?" a cowed "Yes" would have been the answer. "And the new self being born?" Silence, for that was only a ray of hope. Indeed, Quodvultdeus assures them that they have begun to enter the gate of life, to exchange the fragile and mortal for the robust and immortal, and now they had the creed and the banner of the cross (vexilla regis) as a remedy against the venom of the serpent.[31] Nonetheless, they were physically and emotionally drained. Grain, they had been ground to flour for the bread. About that ray of hope, Great (Holy) Week and Easter Week awaited them, not to mention that vigil which brought them to the baptismal font. But that is not part of this story.

So much for the target audience—the order of competents. Who were they? Residents of Carthage, city and countryside. It was customary, at least in Hippo, for people to come to the episcopal see for all of Lent and especially for Great Week and Easter Week; they would stay with friends and relatives, and it would have been no different in Carthage.[32] They were Latin-speaking, as is obvious, but many would have been Punic-speaking, and some Berber-speaking.[33] And their culture was largely Roman provincial—at least since the rebuilding of Carthage three hundred years earlier. Yet the cultural air they breathed was distinctively Punic, particularly in traditions and religion.[34] Although the competents may well have included some of patrician lineage and some who were upwardly mobile, especially people of commerce,[35] the largest percentage would have been artisans.[36] Nonetheless, given Quodvultdeus's extended metaphors about fishing, ships and shipping, and agriculture, clearly "farmers" of sea and land were among the competents.[37] Africa, after all, was the granary of Rome, and Carthage was the major port of the western Mediterranean. Finally, some of Quodvultdeus's congregation would have been refugees from both Italy and the other African provinces, fleeing from the Gothic incursions in Italy and the Vandal menace.[38]

Nonetheless, the audience for the homilies was not only competents. As Quodvultdeus clearly attests, the congregation of the faithful were conspicuously present. Scrutiny, renunciation of Satan, and profession of faith, after all, were enacted before their very eyes; and, if Augustine's congregations are any index, to their shouts. The competents, in goatskin tunics, as we said above, with neck bowed, barefoot, and standing on goatskins, were ritual subjects, not part of the audience. In status, occupation, language, and origin, the composition of the faithful would have mirrored that of the competents, save that more of them might have been able to trace their Christian lineage back to the second century, when Christianity made its embattled first appearance in the city. Even so, only about 20 percent of the entire population lived anything like "the good life."[39]

Religious Turmoil

So much for the catechumenate, its liturgy, and the audience. In the creedal homilies one can see and hear a good deal of religious turmoil in Carthage. Paganism reflected the deepest religious roots of the city's culture. Judaism had arrived by the first century BCE in the packs of Jewish traders and was very much alive in the city. Christianity arrived late, entering in and through the Jews of Carthage and Christians emerged as a persecuted minority in the last decade of the second century of our era. By the fourth century Christianity was clearly the dominant religion, but it was a Christianity sharply divided among catholic, Donatist, and Arian Christians, to mention only the major divisions. Pagans, Jews, and Arian Christians all make a center-stage appearance in the creedal homilies.

Jews and Judaism

Recent studies have shown that our knowledge about the size and activities of the Jewish communities in North Africa is slim.[40] Although it is likely that Jews established themselves in and around Carthage in early Roman times (second century BCE), by the third century of our era at least, there were several synagogues and a community that numbered between three hundred and five hundred. If they were organized as were the Jews in Rome, which seems quite likely, they formed congregations with no central authority. Each synagogue would have a council of elders, with two administrative officers and possibly a president of the synagogue in charge of worship.[41] As in the other cities, the Jews of Carthage would have invited hostility because of their distinctive rites, beliefs, and customs.

Nonetheless, their faith proved attractive to enough sympathetic Gentiles to make proselytes. Indeed, Tertullian, who provides the first record of friction between Christians and Jews in Carthage (c. CE 200), begins his *Adversus Judaios* with the report of a contentious, day-long dispute between a Gentile Christian and a Jewish proselyte. He comments that truth became "overcast with a sort of cloud," and he set about to disperse the cloud in the rest of the work by arguing that Israel had failed to adhere to God and had rejected God's grace. As a result, he concludes that the old covenant and its institutions are invalid, replaced by a new covenant and the new high priest foretold by the prophets.[42]

Prior to Augustine, however, there is little or no record of encounters, much less clashes, between Christians and Jews in North Africa. Yet Tertullian inaugurated a long preoccupation in Latin Christianity with the relationship between the synagogue and the church, one rooted in the need to define attitudes and set boundaries between the old and new religions. Although they shared the same religious heritage, and the new issued from the old as child from mother, mutual rejection stood firmly entrenched between the two. The North African silence, however, was broken by Augustine, who had much to say about Judaism, especially in his refutation of the Manichees. He respected the religious integrity of Jewish practice and tradition, arguing that the Jews are the "desk *[scrinaria]* for Christians, bearing the Law and the Prophets, testifying to the doctrine of the church, so that what we honor through mystery *[per sacramentum]* they announce through the written work *[per litteram]*."[43] In short, for Augustine and his heirs, Jews were faithless witnesses who understood the letter of their scriptures but not the hidden, prophetic meaning. Although he saw them as a continuing and vital part of the history of salvation, the bedrock conviction on which Jews and Christians erected the jagged dividing wall between them in Roman Africa was christological.[44]

Quodvultdeus reports what he takes to be the Jewish side: "They are saying [to Christians], 'How is it that you believe in one God? When [you] call God the one whom our fathers crucified, so that [you] adore and worship the crucified one as though he were the Son of God.'"[45] The creedal homilies are replete with his responses. Sometimes they are in the "desk" tradition of Augustine: "O Jews, you bear the light of the Law in your hands that you may show the way to others, and [yet] you shroud yourselves in darkness."[46] More often they employ a rhetoric of degradation, if not vengeance. In the first homily, for instance, he finds the Jewish darkness starting with Herod's slaughter of the "Innocents" (Matt 2:13–18):

> O wicked land of the Jews, you are at odds with heaven. Heaven discloses a sign that the infant be adored; you scour [the earth] that the infant be killed....Look for the little one; indeed, he came for this, to fulfill even your worst intentions....Take vengeance on those who pursue you as a little one; let their little ones die on your behalf. If cruel men arise against you, let their little ones die in your stead. Punish [these cruel men] thus, punish them. Let the children, as yet unable to speak, condemn their parents, let them convict them for their rage.[47]

The "darkness" eventually leads to Judas and the crucifixion. Using *redemptio* in its root sense of price of purchase, he says:

> What did this mad impiety of the Jews achieve? For, not only did they refuse to attend [the marriage of the Lamb]; they furthermore killed the bridegroom. What did the iniquity of Judas, who sold the one by whom he sought to be redeemed, set in motion? Behold, Judas neither kept the price [he received] nor did the Jews keep the Christ they bought. I ask Judas, "What is it that you received?" I ask the Jew, "What is it that you bought?" To the former I say, "When you sold [Christ], at that moment you cheated yourself"; to the latter I say, "What you bought, you could not hold on to." Exult, Christian, you have won in the transaction with your enemies; what Judas sold and the Jews bought, you acquired....[48]

The dividing wall was Christology. From their side of the wall, the Jews were scandalized that Christians believed the crucified one to be divine and worshiped him accordingly. From the Christian side of the wall, the Jews rejected the promised Messiah and killed the Son of God. The Jews of the creedal homilies, however, are the Jews of the first-century Roman Palestine, not of fifth-century Roman

North Africa. They are Herod, the infants, the Scribes and Pharisees, the Sanhedrin, and the hostile crowds of the New Testament all combined into one: the Jew of the homilies.[49] For Quodvultdeus, this is the Jew that walks the streets of Carthage, the Jew of the New Testament. In his study of the patristic background of medieval Christian anti-Judaism, Jeremy Cohen has called this Jew the "Hermeneutical Jew"—one that the Christian theology and biblical hermeneutics of Augustine and his heirs like Quodvultdeus created to meet the church's needs and creed.[50]

Preoccupied with the Jews and Judaism of scripture, the homilies provide next to nothing about contemporary North African Judaism and Jews, save that the vehemence of Quodvultdeus's rhetoric suggests that Judaism was an active external threat to the church. Perhaps what Robert Wilken said about the laws of the Theodosian code applies to Roman Africa as well as to the eastern empire: "From these laws we get the impression of a Jewish community which is numerically large, geographically widespread, a force to be reckoned with in society."[51]

Augustine, however, provides a clue to what might have exacerbated relations in Carthage, when he mentions the Donatist alliance with Arians, Manichees, and Jews. All four put up a united front against the Catholics, who were in the ascendant because of the Theodotian enforcement of Catholic Christianity as the religion of the empire.[52] All four became objects of persecution in 407. Among other things, their property and places of worship were subject to confiscation, a measure that spurred deep resentment and determined opposition.[53]

Pagans and Paganism

Paganism was a different issue, for two reasons. First, paganism was pervasive in Carthage and in Quodvultdeus's audience. It had been, after all, the public religion of the city for centuries. The competents' journey to the baptismal font lay across the rich and ancient landscape of Berber, Punic, and Greco-Roman paganism.[54] With his eye clearly focused on the Berbers (more often called "Libyans," and in Tunisia today, "Tuaregs"), Quodvultdeus addresses the indigenous North African religious culture with its megalithic seam of religious ore:

> By adoring stone that has no life such a person perishes
> by deserting the God who is one's true and eternal
> life....Souls have gone astray through desires both diverse
> and perverse, such that some worshiped the sun, others
> the moon and stars, others the mountains and certain
> trees....[55]

That this Punic-Libyan current was strong may have inspired
Quodvultdeus's animated impersonation of the idols in a colorful
diatribe. He addresses each deity—heaven, sun, moon, sea, and
earth—and has each chide the devotee. In a colorful nautical
response, for instance, the sea says:

> We are not God. For I offer service, as commanded of
> me, when I buoy up the passage of the ship's keel with
> favorable currents, and direct its course by the wind's
> force, so that I bring you to your destined port without
> delay, even if you are hurrying because of avarice. In
> truth, you know that the animals begotten of me have
> been given to you as food. Therefore, since I know my
> place in the scheme of things, why do you abandon your
> place by forsaking the Creator of all things?[56]

By Quodvultdeus's time, however, the religious culture indigenous to North Africa was diverse. There was the Roman civic pantheon with its prescribed rituals: "Jupiter, Saturn, Mars, Juno,
Minerva, Venus and the rest of the monstrosities."[57] But underneath
the Roman *dramatis personae, interpretatio Romana* had taken place, for
the pantheon's functions coalesced in Saturn and Juno Caelestis, the
city's tutelary deities, whose direct ancestors were the Phoenician
Baal Hammon and Tanit.[58] Saturn had become the champion of
African paganism: enthroned as the sun, protector and guarantor of
the city's prosperity, regenerator and fecundator, the object of sacrifice—in short, the Lord and Master. Indeed, as Baal Hammon in
Phoenician Carthage, he was the object of child sacrifice, disclosed
by the discoveries in the Tophet, or open-air sacrificial grounds of the
old Punic city.[59] Caelestis, as Tanit, the "face of Baal," was also an
object of sacrifice; but as Juno, she was the spirit of all women. As virgin, bride, and mother, Caelestis-Tanit-Juno surpassed the lordly

Saturn in popular devotion and came to bear the name *panthaea*, indicating that she encompassed all deities.[60] But in Christian Carthage, *Maria-Ecclesia* displaced Tanit-Juno-Caelestis-Panthaea through what might be called *interpretatio Christiana Romana*.[61] Her elevation as virgin yet mother may well account for the remarkable prominence of Mary as perpetual virgin and ever-fruitful mother in the creedal homilies.[62] For in the cathedral church where Quodvultdeus preached the homilies, Caelestis became the church, a fact strikingly illustrated in his *Liber promissionum*. He describes in detail Caelestis's temple, originally constructed by Emperor Marcus Aurelius and then transformed and consecrated by Bishop Aurelius as his cathedral. Astonished at what he considers God's foreknowledge, Quodvultdeus exclaims: "Something amazing and unbelievable presented itself to our eyes: an inscription in large bronze letters was written on the front of the temple, 'Aurelius, the Pontiff, performed the dedication' *(Aurelius pontifex dedicavit)*—the sanctuary of the two Aurelii, Aurelius, *Imperator*, Aurelius, *Episcopus*."[63]

Neither pantheon nor popular cult, however, exercised Quodvultdeus nearly as much as the culture of paganism, epitomized by the spectacles of Carthage. The lure of the "games" pulsed through the streets, tenements, and villas of the city. Indeed, erection of the circus, theater, and amphitheater constituted the symbols of Carthage's resurrection from the ashes of the Punic war.[64]

For Quodvultdeus, however, they were anything but the signs of resurrection. The chariot races of the circus, the mimes and pantomimes of the theater, and the wild animal hunts of the amphitheater were monumental "fronts" for diabolic enticement and cunning. In short, they were the gladiatorial weapons of the devil—not exactly a new theme in East or West.[65] But in Roman Africa they seemed addictive beyond compare. Augustine, for instance, depicts his friend (and later, fellow bishop) Alypius blinded and enslaved by his passion for *nugatoria spectacula*, specifically, for the insanity of the circus.[66] Indeed, once converted from these empty spectacles in Carthage, Alypius would fall again in Rome's colosseum. Augustine reports:

> As soon as he saw the blood, he at once drank in savagery and did not turn away. His eyes were riveted. He imbibed madness....He found delight in the murderous contest

and was inebriated by bloodthirsty pleasure. He was not now the person who had come in, but just one of the crowd....[67]

Drawn from Roman judicial ceremonial, Quodvultdeus's image for the spectacles was a cloud of blinding smoke that makes the spectator forget that he is even human.[68] One has the sense that daily the catechist had to contend with the fanaticism that seized the people. Not only did Carthage produce more mosaics with circus themes than any other city in the empire, but the excavations have revealed a trove of lead curse tablets *(tabellae difixionis)* that sought to wreck the opposing team: "I conjure you up, prematurely dead demon...by the powerful names of Salbal....Paralyze them in their course, destroy their power, their soul, elan and speed...."[69] He probes the causes of this "hippomania" in the homilies. "Whence comes the pleasure that enthralls circus-lovers," he asks. "Could it be the sight and sound of people roaring with mad fury? Perhaps, from a driver cutting off a competitor and crippling his horse? Maybe from a contestant who has actually lost part of his horse?"[70] One senses the blood lust.

And about the theater,[71] Quodvultdeus wonders aloud whether the delight in the theater comes from the explicit sex on stage, or from the sight and peril of the tightrope walker, or from the ingenious contrivances that waft the hero into the heavens or make boys disappear into the wings or that let actors perform in the air.[72] To those who rush to the wild hunts in the amphitheater he puts the question whether it is the two hunters, poisoned by desire, grappling with nine bears that incites their lust? Or perhaps it is the grim producer saddened because one of the hunters, after piling up bear corpses, escapes unharmed?[73]

Whatever the inducements, circus and amphitheater were "rat-traps" *(muscipulae)* by which the devil again chained in servitude those whom Christ, who had taken captivity captive, had freed. But in renouncing Satan, had the bishop's flock stopped flocking to the spectacular pomps and service? The circus in Carthage held forty to forty-five thousand people, and it continued to flourish until the seventh century.[74]

Heretics

The Jews were allied against the Catholics, and the pagans enveloped their culture. What about the heretics—who were they and what was their threat? Perfidy was the accusation. As Quodvultdeus saw it, the Jew paid a price (to Judas) for "Christ to be killed and then pierced his side," but the heretics, "nourished from the breasts of mother church, mutilated his whole body."[75] They sliced up the unity of the church—the very charge that Augustine made against the Donatists; thus, one reasonably might expect them to be Donatists.[76] Yet repeatedly we hear in the homilies that they are "Arriani." Unfortunately, the name does not help, since by the mid-fourth century Christians called Arians wore coats of many colors and spoke in different tongues: Greek-speakers from the East and Latin-speakers and Gothic-speakers from the West. Carthage's Arians were clearly Latin-speakers with some Gothic-speaking westerners.[77]

But we must turn to the homilies, especially to *De symbolo* 1 to be specific about their identity.[78] The Father, they asserted, is the greater *(maior)*, the Son, the lesser *(minor)*, and the Spirit, considerably more inferior *(multo inferior)*.[79] The reason for this hierarchical subordination, we learn, is that only the Father is omnipotent—only he exists from himself—thus, neither the Son nor the Spirit is omnipotent, nor, for that matter, is either eternal or co-equal with the Father.[80] Rather, their argument ran, the scriptures depict Father, Son, and Spirit as distinct and individual entities—*personae* in the sense of hypostases that bespeak "different ranks *[dignitates]*, separable and unequal ages *[aetates]*, greater and weaker powers *[potestates]*...."[81]

This doctrine of hypostatic differentiation and subordination is best seen when Quodvultdeus comments on the article about the Holy Spirit in *De symbolo* 1. His point of departure is the baptismal account in John 1:32, where John the Baptist sees the Spirit descending in the form of a dove:

O Arian Heretic, when you hear or read these passages, that the Son is glorified, that the Holy Spirit was given in the form of a dove from heaven, are you not awed by this authority? Your carnal thinking and the fantasy [induced] by the evil spirit that works in the sons of the disobedient conclude that the Father is greater, because he was not seen, that the Son is less, because he was seen as a human, that the Holy Spirit is much less, because he appears in the form of a dove. For, by wrong-headed reasoning you say to yourself: as much as the visible differs from the invisible, so much does the Son differ from the Father; and as much as the form of man differs from the form of dove, so much does the honor of the Son differ from the honor [accorded] the Holy Spirit.[82]

The city's Arians argued that the proportional inferiority of the Son and of Holy Spirit is revealed in scripture by the visibility of the Son as human and the Holy Spirit as dove. But beneath the argument's cloak is the more telling biblical argument: sending and being sent. Although implied in *De symbolo* 1, Augustine makes the Arian argument explicit in *De trinitate:* The Homoians argue that the one who sends is greater than the one who is sent; thus, as scripture testifies, the Father is greater than the Son, and the Spirit, greater than the Son.[83]

Although Augustine and Quodvultdeus both speak of "substance," the latter uses the term twice in this first homily, and then only to chide the Arians because they propose different substances of the Father, of the Son, and of the Spirit; they are separable and, therefore, three gods.[84] The Arian polemic rehearsed in the homily is almost wholly based on biblical texts and interpretation—reasoning about scripture rather than about metaphysics. Indeed, Quodvultdeus echoes Augustine's biblical approach etched in the first four books of *De trinitate,* devoted to the Trinity in scripture; only in the fifth and sixth does Augustine turn to "answer the enemies" of the faith through speculative theology.[85] However, the Arians whom Augustine has in view are the Latin-speaking Western Homoians he encountered in Milan and against whom Ambrose wrote *De fide ad Gratianum.*[86] Indeed, Homoian theology had a rich and diversified presence in the West among Goths evangelized by Ulphilas (d. 383) and among Italians like Auxentius (d. 374), Ambrose's Homoian predecessor in Milan who laid claim to Ambrose's basilica.[87]

This was the Homoianism that came south to African shores and appears as the *Arriani* of the creedal homilies. They sought eagerly to validate their understanding of the Father, Son, and Spirit "according to the scriptures" rather than according to the philosophers. But reasoning about scripture was not all; there was Homoian practice as well. They recruited in Carthage by promising much: "Come...I will defend you," Quodvultdeus's recruiter says, "if you are in need, I will feed you; if naked, I will clothe you. I will give you money...."[88] In the very next sentence we learn that the recruiters pressed money on some potential converts and persuaded others by naked force—not exactly unheard of among Catholics, Donatists, Goths, and finally, Vandals. But of more direct concern to Quodvultdeus is the fact that Homoians showed little inclination to tolerate other points of view once they had obtained power.[89] One thing further: Quodvultdeus's Arians rebaptized Catholics[90]—not surprising if, as we know from Augustine, Arian Goths from Italy had come to North Africa. The Homoian Arians in Italy (especially in Milan) denied the validity of the Catholic baptism, holding, like the Donatists, that baptism was valid only if administered by one with proper intention and status in the true church.[91] Homoians and Donatists, it turns out, had much common ground.

In summary, the religious currents that caused turmoil in Quodvultdeus's congregation and provide the cultural and religious setting of the creedal homilies were three. The first was Judaism, a strong adversary of the church for both christological and political reasons. Jews found offensive Christian belief about Christ's divinity, and by allying themselves with pagans, Donatists, Manichees, and Arians, they actively resisted the imperial religious coercion encouraged by the Catholics. The second was a distinctive Greco-Roman paganism built on indigenous Punic-Libyan religion, which expressed itself in devotion to Caelestis-Juno and Saturn and pervaded popular culture, especially in the spectacles. The third was Homoian Christianity, which insisted on a proportional subordination of the Son to the Father, and of the Holy Spirit to the Son, and aggressively recruited among catholics, whom they rebaptized.

Nonetheless, there was further turmoil on the horizon, to which Quodvultdeus would shortly address himself. In practically no time, the Vandal cloud would engulf Carthage, the bishop, his clergy, and his audience. Victor of Vita records the result: "In the midst of the Vandals our people were quite unable to breathe."[92] But some survived the ordeals Geiseric had in mind. Indeed, Emperor Valentinian

III (425–455) arranged that Deogratias be consecrated to fill the Carthage vacancy caused by Quodvultdeus's death, and he also sold the church's plate to redeem captives taken in Geiseric's siege of Rome the next year (455). When Geiseric died (477), his son Huneric succeeded, ruling for seven years, during which the Catholic bishops were challenged to debate Vandal Arians and were commanded to produce an account of the Catholic faith. Their account stood clearly in the tradition of Augustine and Quodvultdeus.[93] The Catholic church in Carthage survived to live again when Justinian reclaimed North Africa, but in 698, the city would fall for good to the Arabs.

THE SCRIPTURES

The creedal homilies are interlaced with scripture, the over-riding authority for Quodvultdeus, as it was for Augustine. The only other authority to which he appeals explicitly is the creed, which he regards as formulating scripture's essential message. Implicit, however, is the authority of that tradition resident, preserved, and nurtured in what his North African creed calls the "holy catholic church."[94] His argument with the Jews is that they have misunderstood God's revelation, and his argument with the heretics is that they have distorted it. For Quodvultdeus, only the "Holy Church and Bride of Christ" understands and interprets scripture faithfully.[95]

As the homilies make evident, however, the authoritative font of the message is the divine writings *(divinae scripturae)*. God's spokesmen are the prophets, by which Quodvultdeus means all the biblical authors from Genesis through 2 Peter. As God's spokesmen, they recount the history of salvation. Like his mentor, Augustine, Quodvultdeus insists that the biblical authors be read literally, but that their words bear a spiritual sense. When reflecting on the account of Christ's crucifixion in John's Gospel, for instance, the words of the account form a transparency through which he sees the axial event of salvation: Christ's virginal birth, the cross as a marriage bed, the birth of the church, and source of baptism and the Eucharist:

Let our Bridegroom ascend the wood of his bridal-chamber; let our Bridegroom ascend the wood of his marriage bed. Let him sleep by dying. Let his side be opened [John 19:33-34], and let the virgin Church come forth. Just as when Eve was made from the side of a sleeping Adam, so the Church was formed from the side of Christ, hanging on the cross. 5. For his side was pierced, as the gospel says, and immediately there flowed out blood and water, which are the twin sacraments of the Church: the water, which became her bath, the blood which became her dowry.[96]

Yet neither Augustine nor Quodvultdeus had at hand a Bible in any medieval or modern sense. Rather, they had manuscripts of individual books and groups of books based on Latin versions of the Septuagint (including books that would come to be called "Deutero-canonical") and the New Testament. These were the "divine writings." These writings had been in circulation since the second century, and there were many versions. Augustine comments that everyone in the early days who got hold of a Greek manuscript translated it, but that the Itala (also known as the African *vetus Latina* or *Afra*) is to be preferred.[97] Eventually a North African canon of scripture was promulgated during the episcopate of Aurelius (391-430), but to think of a "received version," would be anachronistic. The earliest Latin Bible comprising all of scripture in a single volume goes back to Cassiodorus and his library at Vivarium near Naples (c. 554). Although Jerome's translation was indeed known in North Africa, Augustine appears to have resisted using it, and Quodvultdeus's biblical citations indicate that Jerome's work had not formed part of his biblical initiation. Indeed, Jerome's translation only gradually circulated in the west, coming to be the received or common text—*vulgata*—only in the seventh century.[98] In addition, as one reads the homilies, one needs also to keep in mind that they are the product of notaries and, as will be clear, subject to the vagaries of Quodvultdeus's memory and the points that he attempts to develop. Like his predecessors, he adopts and adapts.

Translation

The translation of the homilies that follows is based on the critical edition published by Réné Braun in *Corpus Christianorum, Series Latina* in 1976 (CCL 60.305-63). It attempts to be as literal as late antique Latin and inviting English permit. Among the trials of the translator is the challenge to preserve Quodvultdeus's oral and direct address, together with his allusive, alliterative, and argumentative late antique language and rhetoric. Like Augustine, he was a man steeped in the thoroughgoing tradition of rhetoric in Carthage.

THE FIRST HOMILY ON THE CREED

INTRODUCTION

1.1. In return to the One "who gives abundantly to all and does not reproach anyone" [Jas 1:5], we have taken up for Your Holiness the duty to discuss and explain the meaning of the rites, whether those performed last night or the creed now before us.[1] "For he is generous to all who call upon him" [Rom 10:12]. 2. He is surely able to assist our purpose, making your prayer on our behalf acceptable. And so pay heed, you who long for God's word through faith, as if seeking food from which God grants you growth.[2] 3. For at this point you have not yet been reborn through holy baptism; rather, through the sign of the cross you have now been conceived in the womb of the holy church.[3] Thus, let this mother act first to feed with proper food those whom she carries that after birth she may rejoice at having taken up the very ones whom she spiritually nourishes.[4] 4. What is it, most beloved, that was celebrated around you? What is it that was done last night among you that was not done on previous nights?[5]

THE PIVOTAL RITES

5. The scrutiny was performed on you in the following way: From concealment you were each presented before the entire church, where, with your head—once erect in pride and malice—bowed, you were standing barefoot on goatskin.[6] In this way the proud devil was rooted out of you, while the humble Christ, Most High, was invoked over you. 6. And so all of you were humble of demeanor and humbly you were pleading by prayer, chanting psalms, and saying: "Probe me, Lord, and know my heart" [Ps 138:3].[7] 7. He has probed, he has examined, he has touched the

hearts of his servants with fear of him; by his power he has caused
the devil to flee, and he has freed his servants from the devil's
dominion. 8. Here the poor are not treated one way, the rich
another, the master one way, the slave another, for "there is one
entrance for all into life" [Wis 7:6]; and if [this ritual egalitarianism]
is [the case] in this fragile and mortal life, how much the better will
it be for that immortal and everlasting life?[8] 9. And so the purified
family of the Redeemer, after it had chanted the song of salvation [Ps
138], received the creed as a remedy against the venom of the serpent: so that if, when the diabolic adversary sought again to lie in
wait, the redeemed one will know how he ought to withstand him
with the rite of the creed[9] and the banner of the cross.[10] Armed with
such weapons, the Christian easily vanquishes him, whereas previously the completely unfair devil had wickedly triumphed by evil
oppression. 10. Why had the devil become our adversary, unless for
this reason, that he sees now free those whom previously he had held
captive, that he sees now healed the wounded whom he had felled
with his javelin, that he sees for a second time, clothed in immortality, all whom he denuded by seducing them with sin [see Gen
3:7–19]. In short, he sees that his "rat-traps have been broken and we
have been set free: our help is in the name of the Lord" [Ps 123:7–8].
11. If our help is in his name, let us renounce the devil, his pomps,
and his angels.[11] You have heard this and you have also professed
aloud that you renounce the devil, his pomp, and his angels. 12.
Beloved, see that you publish this profession of yours in the angelic
court. The names of those making the profession are inscribed in
the book of life, not by just any man, but by a higher, heavenly
power.[12] 13. God's finest new recruits, strong soldiers of Christ,
already as you receive the weapons of the rites, you declare war on
Satan; as you renounce his works, you provoke his rage against you
more vehemently. 14. But let no soldier of Christ be afraid, for you
will be putting on Christ himself, so that through him you may
speedily prevail against your adversary the devil.

15. With what weapons does that one also fight? Enticement
and cunning. There are two kinds of his remarkably powerful
weapons to which every soldier of Christ who wants to triumph and
overcome the devil's power must stand up. 16. What are these two
kinds of weapons? Pleasure and fear. Some he captures with pleasure; others he defeats with fear. Let our battle line be strengthened,

and let the arms of the spirit be presented. 17. Let the "chaste fear of the Lord, lasting forever" [Ps 19:9] stand up to fear of the devil. Let faithful prayer not flee before the spectacles[13] of the most degrading pleasure. 18. What has the Christian to fear, when he is admonished so to pray, so to have confidence, so to believe: "The Lord is my helper, let me despise his enemies" [Ps 117:7; see Heb 13:6]. 19. Nonetheless, beloved, you have known the adversary to seize many through pleasure rather than through fear. For why does he daily set before your eyes the rat-traps of the spectacles,[14] the folly of alluring and disgraceful pleasures, save to capture by these delights those he had lost and to rejoice once more that he has found again those whom he had once ruined?

2.1. What advantage is it for us to rehearse such things? You need to be warned briefly about what you ought to spurn and what to love. Beloved, flee the spectacles, flee the devil's most wicked theater seats,[15] lest the chains of the evil one bind you. 2. But if your soul must be entertained, and it delights in being a spectator, Holy Mother Church displays wholesome spectacles for veneration which may entertain your minds by their attraction and not destroy but guard the faith in you.[16] 3. Is someone here a lover of the circus?[17] Does it give him pleasure to see the chariots contending in the circus, people panting with mad fury, someone cutting off the swift contestant, crippling his adversary's horse?[18] 4. The entire pleasure of it is this: to cheer, because one whom the devil conquers now conquers others; to leap up and down and jeer, because the enemy's side has lost his horse, whereas the very one who is delighted by such a spectacle has lost his empty soul. 5. Contrast our holy, healthy, and most agreeable spectacles. Consider in the book of the Acts of the Apostles the man crippled from his mother's womb; although he had never walked, Peter made him run [Acts 3:2–8]—note the sudden health of the one whom you earlier thought infirm. 6. And if you are of sound mind, and if balanced reason and love of the wholesome flourish in you, think about what you ought to look at and consider where you ought to cheer: there where sound horses are crippled or here where crippled people are healed? 7. But if these pomps[19]—the sight of horses, the construction of the chariots, as well as the livery of the charioteer as he stands, driving the horses and panting to win—if these pomps delight you, as I said, he who commands you to renounce the pomps of the devil does not deny them to you. 8. For we ourselves also have our spiritual charioteer, the holy prophet Elijah, who, high astride the four-horse chariot of fire, drove it so far that he scaled the boundaries of heaven [2 Kgs 2:9-12]. 9. And should you want to see the adversaries, whom true power overcame for him, and over whom he flew, and, victorious, over whom he received the palm of highest heaven, remember: "He threw into the sea the pharaoh's chariot and all his power" [Exod 5:14].

10. Perhaps someone else, a lover of the theater,[20] needs to be warned about what one ought to shun and in what to take delight, and, in so doing, he does not lose the inclination to watch but changes it. In the theater lies the fall of morals—to listen to the base, to hear the indecent, to see the pernicious.[21] 11. But let us contrast those spectacles each with the other [spiritual spectacles], that we may, with God's help, drive these things from your hearts forcefully. 12. There the spectators see presented some kind of fabricated god, Jupiter, both an adulterer and a thunderer. But here we look on the true God, Christ, teaching chastity, destroying impurity, preaching wholesome ways. 13. There the same Jupiter is portrayed, having Juno as both sister and wife; here we preach holy Mary, ever mother and virgin. 14. There the visual astonishment is induced in the spectator by the usual tightrope walker; here the astonishment is a great miracle, Peter crossing the sea on his own feet [Mark 14:29]. 15. There chastity is profaned through the vile mime;[22] here lust is restrained through chaste Susannah [Dan 13:8, 45] and chaste Joseph [Gen 39:7, 20]; death is disdained, God is loved, and chastity exalted. 16. The chorus and the pantomime's song there entice the hearer but subvert healthy affection; but what kind of scene ought to be compared to our song, in which one who loves and sings, says, "Sinners have recounted their amusements to me, but they are not according to your law, Lord; all your commandments are truth" [Ps 119:85-86]? For there, make-believe fashions everything. 17. Maybe someone there admires the ingenuity of the inducements to sin, boys playing in the air, acting out all sorts of stories.[23] 18. But consider the games of our little ones. The two struggle in Rebekah's womb: As the elder emerges, the heel of the elder, which has come out of the womb, is grasped by the hand of the younger [Gen 25:22-26]. 19. In their struggle the figure of a great mystery is disclosed, that the younger would supplant the elder and afterwards snatch from him the blessing and his place as firstborn.[24] 20. In these infants, as if

with playmates acting out a great mystery, as I said, the Jews are revealed as rejected in Esau, and the Christians appear as predestined in Jacob. 21. Jacob, as a small chattering child, reveals in himself the many predestined infant children who are received from the womb of their mother by the hands of the faithful, nor do they shake them so that they hang them in air but so that they are reborn in heaven.[25] 22. Therefore, let the mind take delight in those entertainments, let the Christian soul be fed. Clinging to this sobriety of mind, let the soul flee the devil's intoxication. 23. And do not let the contests of the amphitheater entice and lead astray the Christian, for the more avidly such a person is spurred to run to the amphitheater, the slower he is shown to be.[26] But more important, what is displayed there for the spectators that is not dangerous, not gory? There, where, just as Blessed Cyprian says, lethal desire condemns men to the wild beasts for no crime at all.[27] 24. Beloved, do not let that cruel spectacle invite you to watch two hunters fight against nine bears; rather, may it delight you to see our own Daniel conquering seven lions by praying. 25. Discriminate between these [two] contests, Lover of the Spirit, see the two [hunters] poisoned by desire; think of the one [Daniel], innocent and full of faith.[28] Think of those two having offered their souls to the beasts for an earthly reward; see that one chanting in prayer: "Do not hand over to the beasts the souls of those who confess you" [Ps 74:19]. 26. In that other spectacle, the producer is distraught if the hunter who kills many of his beasts escapes unscathed; in this spectacle of ours, the battle is fought without the sword; Daniel is not wounded nor the bear killed.[29] Indeed, the battle is waged in such a way that the king [Cyrus] is astonished and changed, the people are cowed, and the enemies utterly perish. 27. Our admirable spectacle—entirely wonderful, in which God assists, faith wins power, innocence fights, holiness prevails, and such a reward follows that he who conquered gains as well, and he who yields loses nothing [Dan 14:40-42]. 28. Long for these spiritual shows, come eagerly to church to behold them and to watch in full security, summon your heart's attention back from every carnal desire, submit your every concern to God's rule. Then, should the adversary return, he will find nothing belonging to him in you, save that you repudiate him and renounce his pomps. And later, when your liberty has been snatched from his snares, let that abominable one, whom we know is also eager to capture those who are not his, find you empty.

THE CREED[30]

3.1. Believe firmly in God the Father omnipotent [the article of the creed about to be commented on]. We believe in an all-powerful God who, although making all things, has not been made; and, therefore, he is all-powerful, because everything he made he made from nothing. 2. For no matter at all assisted him from which he might display the power of his skill. But from nothing, as I said, he created all things.[31] 3. Indeed, this is what it means to be omnipotent, that not only the end product itself but even its matter is found to exist from him who had no beginning to his existence, and he who is eternal created not what he himself was, but in order that creation might take from him who already was. 4. For everything that exists, exists from him; rather, the Very One not made by anyone exists from himself. Thus, the Unmade made what has been made; the Uncreated created creation. Indeed, it is he who constituted the powers through orderly arrangements by a hierarchy of being appropriate to these very creatures.[32] 5. Surely, from the standpoint of a given power, an angel or a human can be called powerful, but can either be called omnipotent? 6. A king or emperor can be called powerful, because he can do whatever he wills. But no one who is rational would dare to call himself omnipotent, for if someone wanted to praise that person by such flattery, in making such a mistake, he begins to deceive both that person and himself. 7. For in what sense will he dare call omnipotent one whom he sees wanting to live to the full a life with death standing at its end? If he is omnipotent, he will not die; if he is omnipotent, he will not be cut off by death. However, if death puts an end to him, death itself will demonstrate that he was not omnipotent. 8. Therefore, no one will make bold to call any creature whatsoever omnipotent, whether celestial or terrestrial, save only the Trinity: the Father, and the Son, and the Holy Spirit.[33]

9. When we say that we believe in God the Father omnipotent, we do not deny, as the Arian heretics do,[34] that the Son is omnipotent, nor that the Holy Spirit is omnipotent. If you deny that the Son

is omnipotent, you also deny that the Father is. 10. But "the Father is greater," they say, and "the Son lesser."[35] Indeed, this is the way it is among humans; this is the way it is in everything that exists, and so you are confused by all that exists. Consider the divine nature; turn your attention to God; think of the eternal one: You are confused without reason. 11. If the Father is eternal, the Son is assuredly eternal. For if the Son existed when he was not the Son, [then] the Father also existed when he was not the Father. If there was a time when the Father was not the Father, he was not omnipotent, since there would be something missing in him when he later became Father. 12. If you assign a beginning to the Son, assign a beginning also to the Father. For the Father is called "Father" by the Son. Moreover, if the Father always was, then the Son always was. And if God is the Father, God is the Son also: Nothing other than God can proceed from God. 13. But if God is Father, God is also Son, and if the Father is eternal, also eternal is the Son. [The Father] did not lessen the [Son] in equality, whom he did not surpass in time nor dignity. 14. Listen to what the Apostle says about God the Son: "Since he was in the form of God," he says, "he did not consider equality with God stealing" [Phil 2:6]. He did not steal because he had [this] by nature. 15. And so the omnipotence of the Father is in the Son and that of the Son is the Father, since the Father is never without the Son, nor the Son, without the Father. 16. We are simply unable to explain this divine nativity by which the Son proceeded from the Father and by which God was born from God without a beginning: outside of time, without a mother, without any kind of frailty, without any lessening of himself. The prophet says, "But about his birth, who will recount it?" [Isa 8:33]. 17. And in fact who can understand or say how he who always exists in the Father was born and never departs from him? 18. As I have said, we cannot properly recount it, yet we ought to prepare our hearts for this very Son, so that, by enlightening and guiding us through faith, he may lead us to the grasp of his truth—and this lest we continue in the darkness of our lack of faith. 19. Lest also, by thinking something about the Son other than that he is what the Father is, the Son admonishes us not by teaching but by rebuking, as he did with Philip, saying: "Philip, he who sees me, sees also the Father. Don't you know that I am in the Father and the Father is in me?" [John 14:9-10]. 20. Thus, just as God was born from God and light from light and day from day, so Omnipotence was also born from the Omnipotent. 21. Indeed, in this our mortal way of birth he who is a father was at some point not a father; and he who is a son is not always a son. For in the course of time the son himself will lose his father, choose a wife, and have children, nor will he be a son but will himself be called a father; and no father before he accepts his son will be called father.[36] 22. Something, therefore, happens in time, which in time it [also] surpasses. But let us not think that this is the case in the divine substance with that eternal generation. For there the Father does not decline and die so that the Son, growing up, acquires the dignity of the Father;[37] [if that were the case], time, which was made time by God himself, would be there.

4.1. However, in what way, heretic, will you make bold to assert that the Son, whom we confess to be equal with the Father, is less? In age? The limitations of time are not there. In divinity? God is Father; God is also Son. In work? All things were made through the Son. 2. To be sure, scripture says that God made the world, just as it is written in the book of Genesis, "In the beginning God made heaven and earth" [Gen 1:1]; but in hearing "God the Father," we also recognize the Son and the Holy Spirit. 3. Perhaps, you say, "God the Father made the world." But listen to what John the Evangelist says: "In the beginning was the Word, and the Word was with God, and God was the Word. All things were made through him, and without him nothing was made" [John 1:1, 3]. 4. See, he says that without the Son nothing was made: for "all things were made through him." If nothing was made without the Son, what did the Father make that the Son did not? About this the evangelist states that without the Son nothing was made. 5. However, if you find that the Father is in the Son as he goes about his work, and the Son is in the Father as he works, which the true catholic faith holds, because the Son is in the Father and the Father is in the Son, then the Son will be found omnipotent, if the omnipotent Father is in him. 6. However, if the Son is not omnipotent, as an Arian heretic might preach, [then] the omnipotent Father is not in him, and the heretic, in the very words of the Lord himself, will be wrong: "I am in the Father and the Father is in me" [John 14:10]. Indeed, let what the Truth says be far from error, and let the Arian, who contradicts Truth, be confounded.

7. Nonetheless, let us demonstrate from the scriptures that the Son is called omnipotent just as the Father is, and thus may both

sound reason and divine testimonies strike the impudent brow of the heretics.[38] 8. The Father was called omnipotent, when the prophet says: "The omnipotent Lord said these things" [2 Cor 6:18]. The Son is also called omnipotent when John the apostle says in the Apocalypse: "From Jesus Christ our Lord, who is, and who was, and who is to come, the Omnipotent" [Rev 1:8]. 9. The Holy Spirit has also been called all-powerful by Solomon, who prophesies: "The Spirit of the Lord filled the whole world, and he who contains all things has knowledge" [Wis 1:7]. 10. Or perhaps he who contains all things is not omnipotent? Yet scripture says that God is a judge, when the Apostle says: "We will all stand before the tribunal of Christ, so that each one may report about those things he has done through the body, whether good or bad" [2 Cor 5:10]. 11. But when we hear that God is the judge, we understand it to be the entire Trinity. But, O heretic, tell us who this God the judge is, Father or Son? 12. If you say, "He is the Father," you deny that the Son is judge, whom you confess in the creed that he will come to judge the living and the dead. You also contradict the gospel when it says: "When the Son of Man has come in his glory, all the nations will be gathered before him; and he will separate them from one another, just as the shepherd separates the sheep and from the goats" [Matt 25:31-32].[39] 13. In this gospel citation the judge has been so expressly shown to be the Son that the sentence of this very judge was added, saying: "The ungodly will go into eternal fire but the just into eternal life" [Matt 25:46]. 14. But if you, unwilling to oppose such great authority, called the Son judge, will you then refuse to call the Father judge? You answer, "I do not deny that the Father is the judge." How is it that you do not deny it? "Because the Father," you say, "gave the power to judge and the Son received it." 15. Now I see, heretic, what [way] you turn with squinty eyes, where you direct the line of your mind's perverse attention: For you are about to cite for me from the gospel and say: "The Father does not judge anyone but he has given all judgment to the Son" [John 5:22]. 16. "In this situation," you say, "what the Father gave, the Son received; surely he who gives is greater than he who receives. The Father is greater, the Son, less." Your vanity ought not to brag on account of this passage, because divine authority now refutes you from this same passage. 17. You cite, "The Father does not judge anyone, but he has given all judgment to the Son." We are aware that sound faith surely knows how to interpret this. For the Man-Assumed,[40] the very one who was called the Son of God, received the power given by the Father and the Son; for the Son is in the Father and the Father in the Son. 18. Otherwise, heretic, if, according to that perverse teaching of yours, you wished to ascribe this reasoning [about judge and judgment] to such a deity wherein the Son is equal to the Father, I ask you more insistently and press you to answer me quickly, Who is he who was saying to Moses in the book of Deuteronomy: "On the day of judgment I will repay them" [Deut 32:35]? 19. You cannot say, "It is the Father," because, according to the gospel passage already cited by you, "The Father does not judge anyone." Therefore, it is the Son who was saying: "On the day of judgment I will repay them" [Deut 32:35]. Is it the Son? Answer, what are you uncertain about? Did the Son say this or not? 20. So it is not as you say, unless the Son had said, "On the day of judgment I will repay them, because the Father does not judge anyone." Consider what follows in this book, how it challenges you, in what manner it refutes you. 21. For when it had said, "In the day of judgment I will repay you," following that a little, it added, "See, see," it says, "that I am God, and there is no other before me" [Deut 32:39]. 22. Arian, what argument are you pursuing? This is not the way for you to escape. Say, if you dare, that the Son alone said this, and you will deny that the Father is either God or judge. 23. But now convinced, put away animosity, hear the truth, understand that the Trinity is God the judge. Hear that even the Holy Spirit is judge. The Lord himself says in the gospel: "When the Paraclete has come, he will convict the world of sin, of justice, and of judgment" [John 16:8]. 24. What more are you looking for? The same divine scripture demonstrates that the Father and the Son and the Holy Spirit dwell together in man, although as in his temple. 25. In the gospel the Son says: "If anyone loves me," he says, "he will be loved by my Father; and we will come to him, I and the Father, and we will make our dwelling in him" [John 14:23]. Behold, the Father and Son. 26. What about the Holy Spirit? Hear the Apostle: "Do you not know," he says, "that you are the temple of God, and the Spirit of God dwells in you?" [1 Cor 3:16]. Likewise, it is shown that Father and Son and Holy Spirit, together, abandon the wicked. 27. Solomon the prophet says, "Evil thoughts separate from God" [Wis 1:3]. Behold, God the Father abandoning [the] one with evil thoughts. 28. What about God the Son? He continues: "Because wisdom will not enter into the malevolent soul" [Wis 1:4]. For Christ is the power of God and the wisdom of God [see 1 Cor 1:24]. Behold even the Son deserts the malevolent soul, in which the evil thoughts that the Father abandoned, exist. 29. What remains concerns the Holy Spirit. Listen to what follows a little later: "The Holy Spirit of learning," he says, "will flee what is false and will withdraw himself from senseless thoughts" [Wis 1:5].[41] Understand that the Holy Spirit deserts the person without understanding. 30. Indeed, when the Holy Spirit himself was saying these things through the prophet, he was looking ahead to us. Nonetheless, behold disclosed here by the testimonies of the divine scriptures is that, undivided, the Trinity together dwells, together rules, together possesses, together abandons. 31. [It is this very] Trinity, Arians, whom you do not have dwelling in you, because you injure the Son and Holy Spirit by separating and assigning them different statuses. 32. Indeed, even God the Father withdraws himself from the perverse thoughts that are in you. And wisdom will not enter the malevolent soul, since, just as you separate the Son from the Father through your malevolent spirit, so you separate the flock from the head shepherd. And the Holy Spirit will flee falsehood, that is, the fiction of your perverse teaching, in which it is clear that neither Father nor Son nor Holy Spirit abide.

33. Since, therefore, it is a matter concerning the unity of the Trinity—of the Father and of the Son and of the Holy Spirit—we do not dare to speak of three gods, nor of three omnipotents, nor of three invisibles, nor of three immortals, but of one God, about whom the Apostle says: "Glory and honor alone to God, immortal, invisible, and imperishable" [1 Tim 1:17]. 34. Therefore, let us not make up for ourselves different ranks, different and unequal ages, weaker and more ample powers of the Father and the Son and the Holy Spirit, lest, after our Lord and Savior himself destroyed the idols and temples with his power and majesty, the devil fashion them anew in the hearts of Christians. 35. Therefore, this is the Catholic faith: to believe the Father is God, omnipotent, immortal, and invisible; 36. to believe the Son is God omnipotent, immortal, and invisible, according to his divine birth, though made visible, mortal, and less than the angels [see Ps 8:6] according to his assumed humanity; 37. to believe the Holy Spirit [is God] omnipotent, immortal, and invisible, according to his equal divinity, but visible in the form of a dove because of the testimony of the Son [Matt 3:16].

38. Uncompounded unity, inseparable, invisible, unerring, always abiding, always present, everywhere ruling, this Trinity is one God, about whom the prophet David says, "You alone are the great God" [Ps 85:10].

5.1. We believe in his Son Jesus Christ, born of the Holy Spirit from the virgin Mary. Unbeliever, why do you become frightened at this nativity? 2. Were [he] only a man who was born, do not believe it; but if it was God as man, he was born of her whom he chose, since he chose to be born. 3. Better to wonder at the fact that the Word assumed flesh; nor was he altered in the flesh, because remaining God he assumed man. What else makes you wonder? Because a mother gave birth to her creator, because a creature created her maker?[42] 4. So [it was]: The Exalted chose to be born humble that he might disclose majesty through this very humility.[43] The mother, virginity intact, was carrying the Son, and she herself, whom the marital embrace had not enfolded, marveled at the feel of her offspring.[44] 5. But, unbeliever, listen to the prediction and understand the fulfillment. David, as prophet, says: "A man will call her 'Mother of Sion,' and a man was made in her, and the Most High himself founded her" [Ps 86:5].[45] 6. The Most High, who founded her, was made man in her, the same Most High, because he created such a mother, the same Most High, because he formed himself in her: He, in emerging from her womb, at the same time gave her a Son without taking away her virginity. 7. What is the grace of this mother and virgin? What is the grace of this woman, who, not knowing man, carries a son? What is the grace? Listen to the angel Gabriel greeting her: "Hail, full of grace, the Lord is with you" [Luke 1:28]. 8. When the angel greeted this virgin thus, then the Holy Spirit made her fruitful: this woman then conceived a man without a man, then was filled with grace, then received the Lord, so that he who had made her was in her. 9. For it must not be believed, beloved, that, with him already present and protecting her, corruption could dominate her, in whom there was no burning desire.[46]

10. Nonetheless, the virgin mother recognized whom she carried, she knew; let astonishment flee and faith enter. Behold, the one whom she carried is born. He does not yet speak, but awakens the whole world. 11. Heaven cries out, radiant with the light of a new star; earth, distressed by Herod, cries out; Magi, warned, come; Jews, troubled, inquire; [everyone] asks where is he who is everything: The

maker of the world is sought throughout the world. 12. He was being sought, however, not that he might be acclaimed but that he might be killed, for "the world was made through him, and the world did not know him" [John 1:10]. O defiled world, he who would redeem you came, and you have become troubled; when he arranged to liberate you, you then wished to destroy him! 13. O wicked land of the Jews,[47] you are at odds with heaven. Heaven discloses a sign that the infant be adored; you scour [the earth] that the infant might be killed [see Matt 2:13-18]. Heaven announces to you that God assumed man for you, and you wish to do away with him who came to redeem you. 14. Wait a moment!—indeed, he came for this, to fulfill even your worst intentions; but be patient—so that he may gather up his inheritance. 15. Gather, Redeemer, gather: let him not brag who scatters. Punish those who pursue you as a little one; let their little ones die on your behalf.[48] If cruel men arise against you, let their little ones die in your stead. 16. Punish [these cruel men] thus, punish them. Let the children, as yet unable to speak, condemn their parents, let them convict them for their rage. Because in you is no malice at all, let the infants give testimony about your innocence. And those who want you, the Innocent One, to be killed, may it happen that you part their little ones from them. 17. Although it is fitting for you Jews to mourn and to weep for your sons, they do not die just because they are taken from life. The penalty of bereavement is inflicted on you; as for the rest, the glory of immortality is offered to them. 18. You told Herod where he might find the Son of God, so that he might be killed, but [Herod], in killing your sons instead of the Son of God, inflicts the punishment of bereavement on you, as if you were traitors, and, without realizing it, he was making your sons the firstborn sons of God. 19. Thus did that one who, dwelling in heaven, while lying helpless on earth, ridicule you; thus did he, when he turned your evil deeds back on you and made much good come from your evil, mock your fury and that of your king.[49]

20. Virgin Mother, you knew well your son's infancy; recall equally well his boyhood. The gospel speaks:

> His parents departed for Jerusalem with the boy Jesus, it says, to offer sacrifice for him according to the law. When the sacrifice had been offered, as they were returning, the boy Jesus remained in the temple: for he was in dis-

cussion with the elders and scribes, and all were amazed
at the wisdom in him, yet he disturbed many. 21. But
when they went back looking for him, they found him
seated in the middle of the elders, inquiring of and
responding to them. His mother asks of him: "Son, why
have you done this? For behold, worried and anxious, we
have been looking for you." "Why were you concerned?"
he asked. "Do you not know that I must be doing the
things of my Father?" [Luke 2:42–49]

When his mother heard such words from her son, she became afraid
at heart, for he was not talking about a father on earth whom he did
not know, but about him "who made heaven and earth" [Gen 1:1].

23. Let her also recall his young manhood; let her see the many
great miracles, the change of the water into wine. In this first miracle, this woman, who acknowledged that she was a handmaid,
thought she could give orders to her son, as if she were mistress of
the house. "Son," she says, "their wine has run out; do something so
that the water may be changed back into wine" [John 2:3, 5]. 24. And
in order to show the difference between God and man—as man he
was subordinate and as man, subject, yet as God, superior to all—he
said, "What is that to me and you, Mother? My hour has not yet
come" [John 2:3–5]. 25. It is as if he were saying to her: "The hour
will come, when that which was born of you, hanging on the cross,
will acknowledge you and will commend you to his beloved disciple."[50] But in this miracle why did he say "to me and to you?"—"For
the miracle did not come from you, but from him who made you: It
is not your place to give an order to God; rather, it is your place to
be subject to God." 26. The devout mother, who did not take amiss
his admonition—"What is that to you and to me?"—let her see at work
in the other miracles the very God whom she saw to be her son as
he was growing up. 27. Let her see the blind given light, the lepers
cleansed, the lame running, the deaf hearing, the demons fleeing;
and what is better than all these miracles: the resurrection of the
dead. But at this moment let this mother now recognize and stand
in awe of her young son.

6.1. What remains for the young man save as Bridegroom to go
in search of his bridal chamber?[51] Let the Bridegroom embrace the
bride, searched for and found, to be joined to him.[52] He is not only

man, but he is God and man. Let her be sought after who is to be united with him. 2. The kind of woman he was born of, let such a woman be found for him, to whom he gives fecundity as a mother, yet whose virginity he preserves intact. Let the Son of her who remains a virgin take to himself one who will remain a virgin.[53] 3. Behold, the time is at hand; right now, when he grants them the power, let the Jews fulfill his will. Act, Jews, ignorant of the wedding of the Lamb,[54] pay the price or blood money to that evil, no-account Judas. Act so that he who was born of a virgin may be hung from the cross by Pontius Pilate. 4. Let our Bridegroom ascend the wood of his bridal chamber; let our Bridegroom ascend the wood of his marriage bed. Let him sleep by dying. Let his side be opened [John 19:33–34], and let the virgin church come forth. Just as when Eve was made from the side of a sleeping Adam, so the church was formed from the side of Christ, hanging on the cross. 5. For his side was pierced, as the gospel says, and immediately there flowed out blood and water, which are the twin sacraments[55] of the church: the water, which became her bath; the blood, which became her dowry. 6. In this blood the holy martyrs, friends of the Bridegroom, washed their robes, made them white, came as invited guests to the marriage of the Lamb [see Rev 22:14], took the cup from the Bridegroom, drank, and gave their pledge to him. They drank the blood of him for whom they poured out their blood. 7. What did this mad impiety of the Jews achieve? For not only did they refuse to attend, once invited; they furthermore killed the Bridegroom. What did the iniquity of Judas, who sold the one by whom he ought to be redeemed, set in motion? 8. Behold, Judas neither kept the price [he received], nor did the Jews keep the Christ whom they bought. I ask Judas, "Where is what you received?" I ask the Jew, "Where is what you bought?" To the former I say, "When you sold [Christ], at that moment you cheated yourself"; to the latter I say, "What you bought, you could not hold on to." 9. Exult, Christian; you have gained in the transaction of your enemies; what Judas sold and the Jews bought, you acquired. Rejoice, rejoice, bridal church, for had not these things happened to Christ, you would not have been formed from him. 10. Sold, he redeemed you; killed, he loved you: and since he loved you so much, he chose to die for you. Oh the great mystery of this marriage! How great the mystery of this Bridegroom and bride! Human words are not up to explaining it. 11. From the Bridegroom, the bride is born. As she is being born, she is immediately united to him. At the very moment her spouse dies, the bride marries him. At the moment he is joined to his bride, he is severed from mortals. At the moment he is raised above the heavens, she is made fruitful throughout the whole earth. 12. What is this? Who is this Bridegroom at once absent and present? Who is this Bridegroom here and hidden, whom the bride, the church, lays hold of only by faith, and, without any embrace, bears his members daily? Who is this who was thus born, thus spoke, thus died? 13. Who is this infant who terrified the king? the boy who confounded the Jews? the young man who upset Pontius Pilate? Who is this person? Do you want to know? "The Lord of Hosts, he is the king of glory" [Ps 23:10]. 14. If the Lord of Hosts is indeed the king of glory, then he neither feared the Jews when they had come to arrest him, nor the judge, exercising unjust judgment, nor the taunting soldiers, nor the mocking enemies, nor those crowning him with thorns, nor those dividing his clothes, nor the gall, nor the vinegar, nor the cross, nor the lance, nor death. 15. For, as those Jews and Pontius Pilate were doing these things, the Lord of Hosts negotiated our affairs: What he had not stolen, he nonetheless was returning. He did not steal sin, but he accepted death for sin, that he might fulfill what was written concerning him: "What I had not stolen, I must nonetheless give back" [Ps 68:5]. 16. And then, so that you would know that he paid what he did not owe—for "Christ died for us" [Rom 5:6]—shortly he paid out of the purse of his own flesh on the wood of the cross the price for us and gave it to the collector; here instantly he made the thief a confessor [Luke 23:42-43], so that through him he might repair the damage the impious did. 17. Think about the redeemed thief, whom, as a murderer, the devil owned; think also of the Lord of powers, performing a miracle in his very death. At one point, the thief professes [his faith in] him, when Peter was confused; at one point, this one acknowledged [him] [Luke 22:55-62], while that one denied [him] [Matt 26:69]. 18. Could it be that, because the Lord found the thief, Peter, who denied him, was lost? No, not at all! He who poured out the ransom enacted a mystery, showing in Peter that no one ought to presume anything just in himself, and in the thief that no impious person need perish.[56] 19. Let the good be afraid lest one perish through pride; let the bad not despair because of great evil. Let the presumptuous be corrected; let the despairing be gathered in. We know that the great ransom has been paid for us, because the blood of Christ has redeemed us. 20. Let us pursue how we may avoid displeasing such a Master. Note how he loved his servants, and those servants whom he redeemed, he in turn made free. Behold, it is not only that he grants liberty, but he confers brotherhood and also promises an inheritance. 21. Is there something more you want? By coming, he took up your death, by rising he gave [you] his life [Ps 115:12]. Do you want still more? He, the one who was crucified for you, by rising on the third day, raised you above the heavens. He made you a son of God.[57] 22. Is there still something more you want? What will we give the Lord for what he has given us? Before we existed he made us, gave us life, gave us a lifetime, gave us a free will, gave us worldly goods, gave us talent, gave us reason, gave us knowledge, gave all his creation that it might become yours. 23. And we have used these things badly and have grown proud. With the recompense of sin, we have offended the Creator, who gives us such good things freely. We were lost, he found us; we were taken captive, he helped us; we were being led to perpetual death, he freed us. 24. How could he who handed himself over to death for you present you with any less? What will we give back to him? If there is nothing that we can return to him, let us receive from him what we offer him. 25. What Christ asks from you is what he says to you:

> What I have done for you, do this also for me; I have laid down my life for you, now lay down your life for your brothers and sisters [see John 15:13]. 26. Do not fear death, for, although you are not able to conquer it, I have died that you might conquer death, not through yourself but through me. In fact, I died not for my sake, but for yours. 27. Indeed, you have known that you will die, [but] you have not known that you will rise. I have shown you death, which you have known about; I have shown you resurrection, which had not known about.

By believing, love the Risen One that through him you may also rise. 28. We have spoken, and, insofar as [Christ] has given [the ability], we have explained three doctrines [of the creed]: that he was born of the virgin Mary, was crucified and buried under Pontius Pilate, and rose from the dead on the third day. If we were to speak about each one of them, as is fitting, the great length of the sermon would inspire in you disdain rather than delight.

7.1. Since, therefore, we have discussed how the Most High came down for us, now let us discuss how he raised to heaven what he assumed from us, placed it at the right hand of the Father, and gave such an enduring pledge to our faith that his members may be secure in such a Head, and may hope firmly that they may be able to come to him whom they already believe sits at the right hand of the Father [the articles of the creed about to be commented on]. 2. Assumed into heaven, he sits at the right hand of the Father. Please do not think of this sitting as arranged for human bodies, as if the Father sat at the left hand and the Son at the right. Rather, understand this seat and the right hand as power that the man assumed by God into heaven accepted, so that he who had first come to be judged might come again to judge. 3. For the following reason also he ascended into heaven: that faith might take his place. Indeed, the following prediction was made through David the prophet, for he says: "The assembly of the peoples will gather around you, and for this reason return to the heights; the Lord judges the people" [Ps 7:8–9].[58] 4. Surely [David] means that because you have been humiliated in the form of a slave, even to the ignominy of the cross [Phil 2:7–8], some of those who saw you crucified believed, [but] many doubted. 5. On rising from the dead, you return on high and deign to ascend above the heavens, so that through faith the congregation of faithful people may be gathered into one, [and] that faith may lead them to sight. 6. This is the power of your omnipotence, that you are more powerful in these faithful when you are perceived to be absent from them in that Man-Assumed.[59] Besides, through the presence of your glory you never depart from the hearts of your faithful. 7. Further, beloved, consider what he has bestowed who ascended to the heights: he has led captivity captive [Eph 4:8; Ps 67:19]; he has given gifts to humankind. Consider about what he has bestowed. 8. He came wonderfully; he grew up wonderfully; he worked the many miracles we have just recounted. He, Eternal Salvation, bestowed healing on many; he who bore our infirmities[60] cured many and varied infirmities. 9. For then, at that time, he was surrounded by a multitude of people whom curiosity of [their] eyes led rather than faith. Finally, many praised the miracles they saw; others disparaged them. 10. For what, then, is the reason for those uttering disparagement other than that he cast out demons in the name of Beelzebub, the prince of demons [Matt 9:35]? For all that, when he performed such great miracles, he was despised. Not only was he not held in honor, but he was killed besides. 11. At that point, why was it that the multitude [of his followers] was not attracted by his [very] presence, save that everything written about him was being fulfilled? For when these miracles were being performed, [his followers] were already being prepared by him; already their captivity was captured [Eph 4:8; Ps 67:19].

12. Was there expectation that the Savior should ascend and bestow gifts? What gifts? Gifts that the disciples received, which Peter received, that he would die for him [now] gone, whom he denied in desperation when he was present [John 21:18-19]. 13. Consider what the same Peter says in his letter, what he pours out from that gift of the Holy Spirit: "O believers in him whom you do not see," he says, "rejoice with joy beyond telling" [1 Pet 1:8]. 14. Let us also rejoice by believing in him whom we do not see, so that, when we have come to him free from care, we may see him. Moreover, he himself will also come, but not in the same way as he came before.

8.1. For he will come to judge the living and the dead [the article to be commented on]. He will come, so that he, the one who stood under judgment, may judge. He will come in that form in which he was judged, so that [the Romans] may see him whom they pierced, so that Jews may recognize the one whom they rejected, and so that the very one, seized and crucified by them, may convict them.[61] 2. Perhaps, beloved, since the evangelical truth is not silent about the fact that he rose with his wounds, if he wished, he could have wiped away every stain from any of his wounds (but he knew what purpose the wounds in his body served: that he might heal the wounds of doubt in the hearts of his disciples). 3. Perhaps, then, as I have said, just as he showed his wounds to Thomas, the one who would not believe unless he touched and saw [John 20:25], so also he will show them to his enemies. For this reason it is said by the prophet: "They will see him whom they pierced" [Zech 12:10, cf. John 19:37].[62] 4. Let him not speak to them as to Thomas: "Because you have seen, you have believed," but as one convicting them, let Truth say:

Behold the man whom you have crucified. Behold God
and man, in whom you refused to believe. 5. You see the
wounds you have inflicted, you recognize the side you
have pierced. For it was opened because of, and also for,
you, but you did not choose to enter it.[63] You who were
not redeemed by the price of my blood, you are not mine:
"Depart from me into everlasting fire prepared for the
devil and his angels." [Matt 25:41]

6. But let their death advance our salvation. If they disdained him,
let us fear him who will thus come to judge. Since he lives, let each
of us hurry, so that we may live; let us run,[64] that we may be
redeemed by his precious blood, lest, when we are not found among
the number of the redeemed, we remain among the number of the
lost. 7. Here and now while one has life, let this better place be chosen. Now is the time of faith. Moreover, the prophet says, "In hell
who will confess you?" [Ps 6:6]. One who wants to live always and not
to be afraid of death, let such a one cling to life, so that death may
be surmounted by life. Let one who wishes not to be afraid of this
judge's judgment right now call upon him as advocate.

  9.1. We believe in the Holy Spirit [the article to be commented
on]. We believe that the Holy Spirit is God, equal to the Father and
to the Son, since he is at the same time in the Father and in the Son.
How is he in the Father? Listen to the Son: "The Spirit who proceeds
from the Father," he says, "he will lead you to all truth" [John 15:26;
16:13]. 2. How is he also in the Son? After the resurrection, the Son
himself, sending the disciples to preach the gospel, breathed on
their faces and said to them: "Receive the Holy Spirit" [John 20:22].
3. How is he the Spirit of the Father? The Lord himself says in the
gospel: "For you are not the one who speaks, but [it is] the Spirit of
your Father who speaks in you" [Matt 10:20]. How is he also the
Spirit of the Son? The Apostle says, "If someone does not have the
Spirit of Christ, he is not his" [Rom 8:9]. 4. Likewise, proceeding
from the Father and the Son,[65] how does this same Spirit bear witness to the fact that the Son took flesh? John the Evangelist says:
"The Spirit had not yet been given, because Jesus had not yet been
glorified" [John 7:39]. 5. When the Son was glorified, he [the evan-
gelist] says: "The heavens were opened and the Holy Spirit descended
on the baptized Jesus in the form of a dove," he says, "and a voice

sounded, saying, 'This is my beloved Son, in whom I am well pleased'" [John 1:32].

6. O Arian heretic, when you hear or read these passages, that the Son is glorified, that the Holy Spirit was given in the form of a dove from heaven, are you not awed by this authority? Your carnal thinking, [coupled with] the fantasy [induced] by an evil spirit that works in the sons of the disobedient, concludes that the Father is greater, because he was not seen, that the Son is less, because he was seen as a human, that the Holy Spirit is much less than the Son, because he appears in the form of a dove.[66] 7. Indeed, by wrong-headed reasoning you say to yourself, "As much as the visible differs from the invisible, so much does the Son differ from the Father; and as much as the form of man differs from the form of dove, so much does the honor [accorded] the Son differ from the honor [accorded] the Holy Spirit." 8. As someone who thinks these things, you are approaching the abyss of error. For people have never been lacking who think about the human soul what you want to say about the divine substance. Some have proposed that souls are consigned to bodies as deserved punishment, and that they wander around in circles, some coming back here as human and others in the body of some beast or serpent.[67] 9. David the prophet, shattering this idea with a divine voice, says: "The impious walk in circles" [Ps 11:9]. Those who believe or preach such things are the impious. As though God were saying to such a person: "What do you think about the children of men?" [David] added the following, "According to your deception, you have multiplied the children of men according to your measure" [Ps 11:9].[68] 10. But that is a different question, on which it is not our responsibility to delay further. 11. Nonetheless, heretic, since our debate with you is about the form of a human and the form of a dove, about this you say that the Son is greater than the Spirit because of the dignity of his status; just as there is a great difference between the nature of a human and of a dove, that much you wish to be the difference between the Son and the Spirit. 12. I could, indeed, respond to you about the innocence a dove has, which a man does not, but I do not respond, for we would need to talk about the man who came without sin. 13. Still, if it troubles you that the Son took a human nature, it ought also to trouble you that the Spirit appeared as a dove, because this man assumed by the Son of God is called "the lamb" by the divine scripture. 14. For John the

Baptist says,"Behold the lamb of God, behold him who takes away
the sins of the world" [John 1:29]. And Isaiah the prophet says: "As
a sheep was led to slaughter, and as the lamb before the shearer, so
he does not open his mouth" [Isa 53:7]. 15. And John the apostle
says in the Apocalypse: "I saw a lamb standing as if slaughtered" [Rev
5:6]. Tell me, if you can explain, why the Son of God is called a lamb,
and I will also explain about the form of the Holy Spirit as a dove.
16. If you were to tell me: "The Son of God is a lamb because of his
innocence," that is just what I will reply to you about the Holy Spirit:
the Holy Spirit is, then, a dove because of innocence. 17. If Christ is
a lamb because of innocence and the Holy Spirit, a dove because of
innocence, "Hold onto the innocence, and see the equality" [Ps
36:37]. If you understand the unity of the Father and of the Son and
of the Holy Spirit, you see the equality.

18. Even now, then, let catholic doctrine undermine your
empty scaffolds and diverse comparisons about the substance[69] of
the Father and of the Son and of the Holy Spirit. The result is that
the buffeting winds, that is, the divine words and the rain of grace
falling, knock down the building that you construct on sand rather
than rock, and, once down, it becomes a vast ruin. 19. Although we
have known that the full Trinity is invisible to us, let us believe, let
us hold fast. Tell us, heretic, who is he who appeared to Moses in the
flaming fire on Mount Sion, whose back Moses saw—the Lord reveal-
ing himself to him?[70] 20. For when he sought to see the face of God,
saying, "If I find favor before you, show me your face"; to this God
answered: "Climb up Horeb, and stand on the rock, and my glory
will pass before you, and you will see my back, but you will not see
my face" [Exod 33:13, 21-23]. 21. Who is he who promised to lead
the sons of Israel in escape from Egypt? "God promised them," the
book of Exodus says, "in a pillar of cloud, indeed, by day, but in a pillar of fire by night" [Exod 13:21]. Who is this? Is it the Father or the
Son? 22. If you answered, "It is the Father," then the Father was seen
in some form. Moreover, you do not dare say, "It is the Son," lest you
be refuted by Moses' own testimony turned against you: "You alone
are God, and we do not know a God other than you" [Deut 32:39].
23. Therefore, you will say of God the Father that he appeared in the
pillar of cloud or fire. If you will say this of God the Father, recon-
sider for a moment your [usual] way of reasoning, and tell me which
is better, the nature of fire, of cloud, of humans? 24. Were you to say

fire or cloud, you would be ridiculed not only by people endowed with sound reason and undeceived by your empty seduction, but also by the animals in whom, although they have no rational intellect, there is, even so, a natural sense not attributed to fire or clouds. 25. But if you said that the human nature is better, the Son is shown by you to be greater than the Father, since the Son appeared in a man and the Father in a fire. 26. Arians, according to you, this might be said: "As right and true teaching has it, just as the Son is not greater than the Father, because the Son appeared in a man [and] the Father in a fire, so also the Holy Spirit is not less than the Son, because he appeared in the form of a dove." 27. This divine substance of the Trinity, while remaining in itself just as it is, so that it might return what was lost and restore our ruin, revealed itself visibly for human comprehension and for proportioning itself to each individual thing; [in so doing] it did not lose its own unity and equality. 28. God is in the fire, but he is not the fire; the Son is in the man, but he was not only what was seen, he was also what was hidden. For if he was entirely what was seen, what is the meaning of what he said to his disciples: "He who loves me, I also love him, and I will reveal my very self to him" [John 14:21]? 29. Therefore, if he was entirely what was seen, what was he about to reveal? And so, he was what was also hidden. So also the Spirit appeared in the dove, but the Spirit was not the dove. 30. All this, humanity, was done for you. Do not choose to do injury to the one who made you, so that you may profit from that which follows in this holy creed:

10. The remission of all sin [the article about to be commented on]. 1. Do not proclaim him to be less, who leads you to the kingdom of heaven through the remission of sins.[71] If someone comes to baptism without this [catholic] faith, he closes the door of remission against himself.[72] 2. Nor did the fact that our souls were snatched from the burden of sins happen in any other way than this, brethren, that the Father sent the Son, that the Son himself assumed human nature to heal it, and that the Holy Spirit poured out that [saving] gift for no other reason than that we be relieved of the burden of sins. 3. Indeed, the Savior assumed the whole of humankind to heal it, but he disclosed that a fuller cure must be conferred on the soul than on the body. For instance, while the Savior himself was performing certain other miracles while among us, he saw a paralytic oppressed by a long-standing condition. He concluded that his soul first ought to be healed; only then did he think it appropriate to confer health on his body [Matt 9:2-8]. 4. "Son, have faith," he says, "because your sins have been forgiven you" [Matt 9:2]. This great cure ought not to be despised. Whoever desires this cure, internal or external, ought to seek it. "Purify the things within," the Lord himself says, "and those outside will be purified" [Matt 23:26]. 5. Nonetheless, the intent of the Jews was perverse, for they did not follow Christ from faith. Rather, the shifty ones came to him, because, when they heard the Lord saying to the paralytic, "Your sins have been forgiven you" [Matt 9:2], they were craftily preparing a plot. 6. Immediately there was this whispering about their thoroughly evil plan, when he, who looked into hearts, heard them: "Who is this," they say, "who forgives sins? He blasphemes: for no one can forgive sins, save God alone" [Mark 2:7; Luke 5:12; Matt 9:3]. 7. But to prove to them that he is God, he showed them their wickedness and at the same time demonstrated his power, saying to them: "What evil are you thinking in your hearts? What is easier to say, 'Sins are forgiven you,' or to say, 'Get up and walk?' 8. But that you may know that the Son of Man has power on earth to forgive sins (he said to the paralytic), 'Get up and take your pallet, and go into your house.' And immediately he got up, took his pallet, and left" [Matt 9:4-7]. 9. Oh! How much better for him, if, after accepting forgiveness of his sins, he did not get up from his bed to sin again, but, free and secure, got up from the tomb to enter true life! 10. For what was said to him, dearly beloved, was not without meaning: "Take your pallet and go into your house." For the Lord wished to heal him within, so that he might not labor further. 11. What else does "Take your pallet" mean, if not, "Take back the burden of your sins"? For your shoulders will not be free; you will carry what presses down on you, while you will be bent under a burden; with head now free you will be weighted down again by slavery. 12. "For everyone who commits sin," says the Lord, "is the slave of sin" [John 8:34]. Were that paralytic, with his sins remitted, to have departed this life [at that moment], he would have received full freedom. 13. But because he was allowed to live afterwards, even if he did not sin (a fact difficult to believe), he was much tested, because this entire life is temptation.[73] 14. And so, beloved, whoever believes with fidelity, and also embraces and holds without wavering in this profession of their faith, in which all sins were remitted, let them shape their will according to the will of God.

15. Thus, if, after baptism, God deemed them worthy to remain in this life for only a little while, let them not rest from praying and saying: "Be my help, do not desert me" [Ps 26:9].[74] 16. If, moreover, God thought it fitting to call them to himself, freed and cleansed from the dregs of sin, let them without hesitation and sadness go to him, with whom and through whom they also begin to reign. Nor should they fear the chariot of death,[75] in which the very one who calls first ascended. 17. For just as by rising he brought himself to the Father, so also, he who came down to earth without departing from heaven to summon you, he will bring you back before the Father by resurrection.

11.1. In the resurrection of the flesh [the article to be comment on]. Let us hold firmly to the resurrection of all flesh, that is, of every rational creature. This is the high point of our faith, the one that separates us from unbelievers. 2. Nor is it permissible for us to discuss [the resurrection] of animals and other living beings, in whom the image of the Creator was not inscribed. Indeed, we know that all these were created for our use. 3. Let someone read what the Lord said to the man and woman when he formed and blessed them. He will find it written in the book of Genesis thus: 4."God made man in his image; he made them male and female and blessed them saying: 'Increase and multiply, and fill the earth, and rule it; and have power over the fish of the sea, over the animals of the earth, over the birds of the heavens'" [Gen 1:27–28]. 5. All these were created, then, to aid our weakness, as I said. But just as neither our tendency to corruption nor our weakness rises together with us, so it is with those things that are needed now because of our weakness.[76] 6. Paul the Apostle speaks about what our future bodies will be like: "It is sown corrupt, it will rise incorrupt," he writes, "it is sown in weakness, it will rise in strength; it is sown in reproach, it will rise in glory; it is sown as a fleshly body, it will rise as a spiritual one" [1 Cor 15:42–44]. This incorruption, power and glory, and living spirit will make us equal to the angels of God, as the Lord thought it proper to promise [see Matt 22:30], 8. so that we may live with them in eternal life in one immortal and eternal homeland. In that homeland our eternal life will be Christ himself: "For he is true God and life eternal" [1 John 5:20].

12.1. In this sacred creed it then follows that after the resurrection of the flesh we should also profess belief in eternal life.

Corruption will no longer have dominion over us as we live in immortality and dwell with Eternal Life himself. 2. Nor will we need clothing, for there we will be dressed in immortality; nor will we lack food when we have the Living Bread that came all the way from heaven to earth for us; for he will satisfy our souls with his presence [John 6:33, 50–51, 59]. 3. Nor, with the Fountain of Life present, will we lack drink.[77] For he will satiate us with the abundance of his house, and he will provide water for our hearts with the torrents of his delights [Ps 35:9]. 4. We will not suffer from the heat there, for our refreshment is there, the one who sheltered and shelters us under the shade of his wings [Ps 35:8]. 5. We will not suffer from the cold there, for there is where the Sun of Justice is. He it is who warms our hearts with his love and who gives light to our eyes with the rays of his divinity, so that we will see the divinity and equality of the Father and of the Son and of the Holy Spirit. 6. We will not get tired there, for our Strength will be with us, the one to whom [even] now we say, "I love you, Lord, my strength" [Ps 17:2]. We will not sleep there, for there is no darkness there that can blot out everlasting day. 7. No commerce, no slavery, no labor will be there.[78] And what are we going to do there? Perhaps what is written [yields the answer], "Be still and see that I am the Lord" [Ps 45:11]. 8. This leisure of contemplation itself will constitute our activity, so that we delight to contemplate and contemplate to see with delight. 9. To see what? "The good things of the Lord" [1 Cor 2:9]. What good things? We will be able to express what "neither eye has seen, nor ear heard, nor arises in the heart of man" [Isa 64:4]. 10. We will be able to explain how "God will be all in all" [1 Cor 15:28]. We will be able to explain how the Son himself, "when he will have handed over to God the Father the kingdom" [1 Cor 15:24] (that is, the holy assembly of the faithful), will not abandon his assumed and fully glorified human nature, lest he delay showing now to the faithful that glory which he had with the Father before the world was made. 11. Can we grasp how the entire church as bride, composed of men and women, is transformed into the perfect man and receives such manly dignity, yet in such a way that [the church] does not lose the name "bride"? 12. Can we understand how the risen bodies of the saints travel from one glory to another?[79] 13. Can we explain where virgins follow Christ, why it is that nonvirgins are unable to follow, and where (I do not know) he who dwells everywhere as a solitary leads these [virgins], yet does not desert those who are not virgins?[80] 14. Who, encased in this very same body dares to say anything, when Paul the Apostle did not feel up to explaining them—Paul, who in his own body [and] with the help of grace, felt strong enough to ascend all the way to the third heaven [2 Cor 12:2–4]. 15. Let us not be curious to investigate what the apostles were unable to express. And certainly let no one try to find out from me what I know I do not know, unless, of course, such a person learns that he is unaware that he wants to know what cannot be known. 16. But through faith and patience and Holy Mother the Church let us hope to receive whatever Christ thought it proper to give to great and small alike.

13.1. Holy church [the article to be commented on], in whom the entire authority of this mystery has its boundaries—mother and virgin, chaste in body, fruitful in offspring, declared earlier to be bride of Christ.[81] With devotion she nourishes her children, whom she strives zealously to signify as worthy of God the Father.[82] 2. Good children, love such a marvelous mother; good children, do not turn your back on the one who seeks you out daily; repay her by loving the one who loves you. She is great and of such nobility that she is a queen fruitful in offspring.[83] 3. Do not allow her to suffer or to be weakened from the insults and plots of either evil children or worthless servants.[84] Defend the cause of your mother; display her magnificent dignity. 4. Do not permit the worthless servant to abuse the mistress. Do not permit the Arian heretic to revile the church. He is a wolf, recognize it;[85] he is a serpent, dash his head.[86] He flatters, but deceives; he promises a lot, but defrauds. 5. Come, he says, I will defend you; if you are in need, I will feed you; if naked, I will clothe you. I will give you money, I will arrange it in such a way that a person may receive something every day.[87] 6. O evil wolf! O wicked serpent! O wretched servant! You scorn your mistress, you assail your true mother;[88] in rebaptizing the Catholic, you foreswear Christ;[89] and, what is the rock bottom of your craftiness, some you compel with force, in order to destroy them, on others you press money which results in their death.[90] 7. Heretic, are you not really clothing the naked, in order to strip from within one clothed with Christ? Are you not really feeding the hungry, in order to take away the heavenly food of the soul? 8. Are you not giving money for this reason, that those wretches may sell Christ for the purpose of rebaptism, just as Judas once sold Christ to the Jews for the purpose of crucifying him?[91] "May your money go with you to perdition" [Acts 8:20]. 9. Heretic, you do far worse than the Jew did. For behold, although the Jew [Judas] was paid a reward for the purpose of killing Christ, and then only once pierced his side as he hung on the cross, still, he preserved his whole body intact. 10. But you, indeed, pay money every day with the result that you cut off different bodily members of the One who sits in heaven. 11. But may you, beloved, who have been nourished from the breasts of Holy Mother the Church in the beginning and have been weaned by her to solid food, remain dwelling in her. 12. If any one of her [children], who has borne either a discipline or an admonition with bitterness and has departed angry, may such a one acknowledge her as mother and return to her.[92] For her part, she freely accepts those whom she seeks out and rejoices that a child who was lost has been turned back. 13. Nonetheless, although she rejoices much over the one who was lost and has been turned back, she does not cease proclaiming the worth and steadfastness of those children who stay with her to the end.

THE SECOND HOMILY
ON THE CREED

INTRODUCTION

1.1. You have come to know that the mystery of the creed, which, as required, you have fixed in your memory as your salvation commanded,[1] is the foundation of the Catholic faith built by the hands of the prophets and apostles; on it the building of the church has risen. 2. The building is truly God's house, and you are the living stones which constitute it. Thus, the Apostle writes to believers: "Do you not know, he says, that you are the temple of God, and the Holy Spirit dwells in you?" [1 Cor 3:16].[2] 3. But also Peter, speaking to believers, says, "As if living stones, you are built into a spiritual house" [1 Pet 2:5].

THE PIVOTAL RITES

May whoever seeks to be part of this building renounce the devil, his pomps, and angels.[3] 4. The pomps of the devil are all sorts of illicit desires that defile rather than ornament the soul, for instance, carnal pleasures, lust of the eyes, and worldly ambitions [see 1 John 2:16].[4] 5. Illicit desires pertain to the ardent longing of the flesh; lust of the eyes pertains to the trumpery of the spectacles; senseless pride pertains to worldly ambition. Such is the case when a cloud of smoke billows up, so that the magistrate, as he hands down a judgment about a person, does not remember that he himself is a human being.[5] 6. But he who wishes to conquer the world, let him conquer these three things that are in the world, and in so doing he also conquers the one who has deceived the world by seducing it through pride.

2.1. After a person has thrown out the worst of usurpers by renouncing the devil, however, let him welcome the best of masters;

let him believe in God the Father Almighty (and the rest) [the article about to be commented on].⁶ 2. To believe and to understand
God is the great gift of grace, for what does the prophet say? "Unless
you have believed, you will not understand" [Isa 7:9]. Let us believe,
then, so that we may understand, but let us pray so that we may
deserve to understand what we believe.⁷ 3. For sins and their author,
the devil, have separated the soul from God: in following the
seducer, the creature deserted his savior. 4. Much ruin has resulted:
the soul strayed from the truth to worship idols in place of God and,
in deserting him by who everything was made, adored the very
things which he made. 5. For by adoring stone that has no life, one
perishes by deserting the God who is his true and eternal life.⁸
Hence every error; hence the desertion of the good; hence pagan
worship and the perversity of heretics.⁹ 6. Souls have gone astray
through desires both diverse and perverse, such that some worshiped the sun, others the moon and stars, others the mountains,
others stones and certain trees, with the result that each one believed
that he had found for himself not God the helper but the devil, the
deceiver.¹⁰ 7. And so, in these diverse ways the soul has wandered
from its creator, with the result that everything God had given for its
use the soul worshiped as God. Have not all things been created for
man? 8. May whoever reads the sacred scriptures also discover that
God said to man, whom he formed from the slime of the earth,
"Increase and multiply, both fill the earth and rule over it; and have
power over the fish of the sea and the birds of the air, and the cattle
of the fields" [Gen 1:28; cf. 8:17; 9:1-2]. And further on a little:
"Behold," it says, "I have given all things to you for your use and for
food" [Gen 1:29]. 10. Moreover, the very nature of things, coupled
with the works of the world itself, convince unbelievers about their
condition as slaves, especially since they do not want to read the
sacred scriptures. In rebuke of the perverse soul the scriptures say:
11. "What is this, unhappy soul, that you wander from me, and, having become degenerate, you forgot him who made you so great—you
for whom so beautiful a home, heaven and earth, was built without
any prior merits of your own?" 12. The elements answer by their
works, with each proclaiming its distinctiveness and demonstrating
its artifice. 13. Heaven cries out: "I am not God: for if I were God,
no cloud could overshadow me nor would darkness obscure my light;
but light whole, undiminished, and uninterrupted would have con-

tinued on, just as that true light lasts which created this temporal light in me for you."[11] 14. The sun also cries out:

> O man, why do you worship me as God, whom you see bounded by rising and setting? God has neither a rising nor a setting: so, by forsaking him you have run a great risk. 15. You think that I am great and wonderful: but I know that I hate having him over me who created both you and me. 16. Moreover, when my role of giving splendor and warmth has deserted you, why do you come to worship me in God's place, save that you do not know how to worship the true God?

17. So also the moon and stars offer the same kind of statement: "Do you not see," they ask, "O man, that we make space dark with night, and that light prevents us from crossing the established boundaries which the omnipotent Artificer set for the comfort of your sleep? 18. We are not God: we refute your error by serving as your punishment."[12] 19. The sea and everything in it proclaim:

> We are not God. For I offer service, as commanded of me, when I buoy up the passage of the ship's keel with appropriate currents, and direct its course with the force of the winds, so that I bring you to the desired port without delay, even if you are hurrying because of avarice. 20. In truth, you know that the animals begotten of me have been given you as food. Therefore, since I know my place in the scheme of things, why do you abandon your place by forsaking the Creator of all things?[13]

21. The earth exclaims:

> Well, then, O man, why do you ascribe the name of divinity to me? For you do not know what I am, because you have forgotten who you are. You do not know the stuff out of which you are made; you do not realize that you are my slime, fashioned from me but, unlike me, with a soul. 22. Among all the animals begotten of me, you do not realize that only you (just below God) have been constituted

master of the world. You did not understand aright. Although you were in a place of honor, you did not realize that you were [still] likened to mindless beasts of burden—and you have become like them [Ps 48:13].[14]

THE CREED

3.1. Beloved, for us to whom it was given to believe, however, let us not believe that God is the sun nor king of heaven, nor in the sea, or its king, Neptune, or someone else, whom vanity rather than truth fashioned, nor in the earth and Pluto. 2. Rather, let us believe in God the almighty Father, creator of the universe, king of the heavens. For he who willed to make everything from nothing rules what he made. 3. Those immortals of yours, who have been commended as beings higher than we are—they are not, therefore, gods, for they can be both understood and seen with these eyes of ours. 4. In addition, the others whom the empty-headed honor with empty worship—Jupiter, Saturn, Mars, Juno, Minerva, Venus, and the other monstrosities—they are not good deities but evil names; even their literature proclaims the fact that they were mortal men, who take delight in such errors.[15] 5. But let our sacred literature propose a different sort of God; hear Paul the Apostle: "May honor and glory be, he says, to the immortal, invisible, unchanging, only God" [1 Tim 1:7]. Our God is not seen by the eyes of flesh but by the eyes of the heart; he is seen in eternity not time. 6. But the pagan says: "Show me the one you worship." I reply, "I, indeed, have just the kind of God to show you, but you do not have the eyes to see." 7. For the Savior says, "Blessed are the pure in heart; because they will see God himself" [Matt 5:8]. Does the heart impure and shrouded in darkness seek to see God? 8. "The light illumined the darkness, but the darkness did not comprehend it" [John 1:5]. Can it be that, because the blind person does not see, the light does not shine? 9. If you had known, O unbeliever, how to say to the true God, "Illumine my eyes" [Ps 12:4], like us you would now see through a glass darkly, so that you would then see face to face [1 Cor 13:12]. 10. If you understood the Artist from his works of art, you would easily infer the Creator from his creatures. Were you to have experienced great terror in yourself because you could not fully fathom yourself, you would have become aware of the God who made you. 11. Since your soul sees everything through your flesh, you do not see your soul. But if [for the sake of the discussion] you see your soul, tell me of what sort it is or how large: 12 whether square or round; whether smooth or rough; whether hot or cold; whether of any color, or lacking all color. I see, you fail to show me of what sort your soul is; you cannot. 13. Behold, your soul is immortal, and it gives life to your mortal flesh. Your soul, I say, is immortal from two standpoints. If it believes, it is immortal for living; if it does not believe, it is immortal for punishment. 14. We believe, therefore, that God is immortal and invisible; not the one whom you unbelievers have fashioned as a god—both an adulterer and a thunderer—rather, the true God, maker and ruler of the whole world.

4.1. We hold that his son is Jesus Christ promised in times past through the prophets, and we know that the promise has already been fulfilled. Nonetheless, we are required to take this on faith, for we were not present when it was made.[16] 2. The Jews were there then, from whom the Savior chose the apostles and through whom the faith itself has come down to us. Indeed, among these very people in and for whom [the Savior] thought it fitting to be born, Isaiah the prophet long ago had predicted, "Behold a virgin will conceive in her womb and bear a son, and you will name him Emmanuel, which means, 'God with us'" [Isa 7:14; cf. Matt 1:23; Luke 1:31]. And in another place: "A virgin will arise from the root of Jesse, and a flower shall grow from its root" [Isa 11:1; cf. Acts 13:23]. "Virgin" signifies Mary, the virgin, and "flower," the son of the virgin, Jesus Christ the Lord. 5. Before these things came about, the Jews read but did not understand them; they began to fulfill what had been promised, yet they did not rejoice; rather they disdained the promises.[17] 6. Christ was born from a virgin like a flower from a shoot, without any semen involved. A small infant is born a great king. 7. Clear signs come beforehand, even the signs of a great king's advent. Angels announce his coming to shepherds. The heavens cry out through a star, as if in a new tongue. 8. The Magi are drawn to him from far away; they come here to adore the one lying in a manger yet already reigning in heaven and earth. 9. At the Magi's announcement of the king's birth, Herod was distressed, and, lest he lose his kingdom, he sought to kill him in whom, had he believed, he would be safe here and reign in that life without end. 10. Herod inquires from the Jews where Christ is to be born. Unlike the Magi, they are also searching, not to adore him, but, once found, to kill him.

> 11. What are you afraid of, Herod, because you hear about the birth of a king? He does not come to topple you but to conquer the devil. Not understanding these things, however, you are disturbed and fly into a rage. And in order not to lose the one you are looking for, you will perpetrate a great cruelty through the deaths of so many infants. 12. None of the grieving mothers' love nor of the fathers' mourning for their sons nor of the son's moaning and tears deter you. 13. To be sure, you slay the little ones in the body, yet fear slays you in the heart; in addition, you think that if you accomplish what you desire, you can live for a long time, even though you seek to kill life itself. 14. Moreover, this font of grace, small and great, who lies in the manger, strikes terror into your throne: through your ignorance of yourself, he accomplishes his own purposes and frees souls from the devil's captivity. 15. He welcomes the sons of his enemies into the number of his adopted children. The little ones unknowingly die for Christ, while their parents mourn the dying martyrs; even though the little ones are not yet able to speak, he enables them able to be witnesses. 16. Behold how he reigns who had come thus to rule. Behold, the Deliverer is already freeing, the Savior is already establishing salvation. But, Herod, ignorant of these things, you are distressed and fly into a rage; and while you rage against the Little One, you already offer him reverence without even knowing it. 17. For this great king, who came that he may gather his flock together here through you and his other subjects here, you have dispatched for him a vast army—many thousands—of white-robed infants, even prior to the coming of the kingdom of heaven. 18. The Apocalypse of blessed John the apostle points to this throng, saying: "I see a great crowd from every tribe that no one could count, standing in God's presence; and they were clothed in white, and palms were in their hands" [Rev 7:9]. 19. O great gift of

grace! What merits of theirs have brought it about that the infants have conquered? They cannot yet speak, but they confess Christ. 20. They are not yet strong enough to fight with their limbs, but they already carry the palm of victory. In what way will you rule, Herod, if you conquer in this way? That Little One [in the manger] has overcome you, not by the hand of strong-armed men, but he conquers by a vast crowd of dying little ones. 21. Do you want to know how you have distinguished yourself from the little ones whom you have slaughtered and for whom you bear responsibility? In so acting, you have hurried them along to their life, lest with their parents they might have killed True Life. You as his agent—he knew well how to use even your evil actions to accomplish this. 22. He delivered their souls from the society of their destructive parents, and he left you alone in your senseless crime. He pursued and pursues his own purposes even through his enemies—both in and through them: For even the ones who were dying were by nature children of wrath, just like the others. 23. But what did grace do for them, if not snatch them from the power of darkness? Christ granted that they might die for him, and arranged it so that by his own blood they would be cleansed from original sin.[18] 24. They were born for death, but immediately death returned them to life.

By the very steps, beloved, with which human nature perished, it was restored by our Lord Jesus Christ.[19] 25. The proud Adam, the humble Christ; through a woman death, through a woman life; through Eve destruction, through Mary salvation. The corrupt one followed the seducer; the pure one bore the Savior. 26. The former willingly accepted the draught of poison the serpent offered, and she gave it to her husband, an act by which they together merited death; the latter, with heavenly grace poured out from above, offered life [as a drink] through which dead flesh could be restored to life.[20] 27. Who is it that has done these things unless it be the Son and Spouse of the virgin? He it is who offers fertility to the mother, but does not take away virginity. What he conferred on his mother, this he has given his spouse. 28. In short, Holy Church, who, without spot, has been united to him, the spotless one, daily gives birth to his members yet is a virgin.[21]

5.1. Crucified under Pontius Pilate and buried [the article to be commented on]—this we believe, and from now on we believe that we may glory in it. "To boast," says the teacher of the Gentiles, the apostle Paul, "should be far from me, unless it be in the cross of our Lord Jesus Christ, through whom the world was crucified to me and I to the world" [Gal 6:14]. 2. In this let us boast; in him let us hope; to him let us cling. For "our old humanity was crucified together with him on the cross" [Rom 6:6]. For unless he were crucified, the world would not be redeemed. 3. This is the cost of our salvation. What Jew and Gentile detest is where the Christian finds salvation. But why does the Jew detest it? The reason, as the Apostle says, is that "since they sinned, salvation [has come] to the Gentiles" [Rom 11:11]. 4. What sin did the Jews commit?[22] They seized Christ, handed him captive over to Pilate, and shouted: "Crucify him, Crucify him" [Mark 15:14–15]. Why? On what grounds? Because he raised a dead man [see John 19:6: Lazarus]. 5. Pilate holds a hearing, finds him innocent, sees the people in a rage, declines to accept responsibility, and says: "I find no case against this man; you yourselves take him and crucify him" [see John 19:6]. 6. When Pilate was saying, "I find no case against this man, take him yourselves," what was he saying except this? "To the judge you have come as if with a culprit, but you have arrested one innocent according to the laws, one in whom you have been able to prove no crime. 7. I would not be a just judge, if, according to your wishes, I were to kill an innocent man, but in turning him over to you I shall not be part of your sedition." "Take him yourselves," he says, "and crucify him according to your law." 8. But to Pilate they say: "We know that the culprit is worthy of death." Blind in heart if not in body, he proclaims what he knows nothing about, and, so that he may allow what they rage about, he pretends to know what he does not. 9. Once again Pilate gives Jesus a hearing. Cast into fear by Jesus' responses, Pilate discovers a plan about how he might turn him over to them. He went out to the Jews and said: "It is the custom that I release to you one [prisoner] during Passover; so, do you want me to release to you the king of the Jews?" 10. They cried out and said: "Do not release him, but Barabbas." Barabbas, as the evangelist tells it, was a notorious bandit. 11. Oh the blindness of the Jews! Oh the fury of the frenzied!

"Do not release him, but Barabbas." What was this except to say: "Let Christ the Savior be killed, because he raised a dead man; let the bandit be released that he may perpetrate another killing"? 12. But shout back: "What are you shouting about, ignorant ones? Let Christ be killed by you and let the Gentiles be redeemed." 13. But that physician of souls, who watched as you worked yourselves into a frenzy, was already entering the sleep of salvation: and so he himself chose to fall asleep for you.[23] 14. Nonetheless, let him say: "I am the physician, you are the sick ones; your grave illness shuns the sleep of salvation. Behold, it is I who sleep for you, so that, when you have contemplated my example, sleeping may delight even you, and I will free you from the punishment of death." 15. He was saying this to and about them, so that, when they have come to believe in him afterwards, he had already known them. Hanging on the cross for them, he asked the Father, saying: "Father, forgive them, since they do not know what they are doing" [Luke 23:34]. 16. Among them was also this madman, formerly called Saul, but afterwards, Paul—at first proud, afterwards humble. As he was working himself up into a frenzy, he turned his back on the sleep of salvation. 17. And the physician, what did he do for him [see Acts 9:1–9]? He prostrated a madman, he raised up a believer; he prostrated a persecutor, he raised up a preacher. Flat on the ground, the madman slept; he rose and became a physician. 18. He began to cure in others the very disease under which he was laboring. Once made a disciple of the heavenly court physician, he himself first drank the antidote compounded of the blood of the crucified, and he promised that it would be drunk by those who love [him]. 19. This antidote, compounded of the blood of the crucified even the kings of the earth themselves have drunk; and those who were persecutors of the church became its defenders.[24]

6.1. The holy gospel depicts the burial [the artcile to be commented on] of this holy crucified one, namely, that he was taken down [from the cross] by Joseph and, once wrapped in linen clothes, was placed with spices in a new tomb [John 19:38–41]. 2. The New Man, begotten of a virgin without any defilement, was placed in a new tomb, one in which no dead person had yet been placed, so that the sanctity of the virginal womb might be honored in every way by the fittingness of the hallowed tomb.[25] 3. On the third day he rose from the dead. As many holy people as you can count have given their opinion here and spoken on this subject.[26] For some, wishing to explain the three days and the three nights, have calculated the first day to include the night preceding the sixth day and the sixth day itself, and the [second], the night of the Sabbath and Sabbath day, and [the third] the night of the Lord's day and the day of resurrection itself.[27] 4. However, others wish to explain the three days and three nights from the sixth day and night—which began at midday—until the Lord's day [itself], on account of this saying of the Lord in the gospel: 5. "For just as Jonah was in the belly of the whale for three days and three nights, so the Son of Man must be in the heart of the earth for three days and three nights" [Matt 12:40; John 11:14, 44].[28] 6. But rejecting both interpretations, we prefer, if you please, a spiritual understanding[29] of the way in which the Son of Man was in the heart of the earth for three days and three nights. 7. Understanding the three days as three ages of the world: before the law, under the law, and under grace,[30] and the three nights as the three deaths, that is, the three dead people whom the Lord, while present in the flesh, raised, namely, the daughter of the president of the synagogue lying dead at home [see Mark 5:21–34], the son of the widow outside the gate [see Luke 7:11–17], and Lazarus, four days in the tomb [see John 11:1–44]. 8. For whence comes death, save through sin, and what are sins save the thick shadows that make the tomb dark as night? 9. Thus, [the three ages] conform to Jesus, namely, the first day is before the law, when sin was concealed, and to this corresponds the night when the dead girl lay in the house, as if she bore sin hidden within her conscience. 10. Let the second day be under the law, when "Do not covet" [Exod 20:17] was addressed to people and sin became public; and that night corresponds to the time when the son of the widow was carried outside the gate, as though the sin of the soul that lies within becomes a public matter. 11. Let the third day be under grace, when the soul sins all the more, since it knows the will of its Lord, and does things worthy of blows even under such a fullness of grace, and deservedly feels shame now before sinners;[31] 12. and to this corresponds that night of the death of Lazarus, lying in the tomb as if he were a soul, foul-smelling and buried by sins. During these three days and nights Christ was in the heart of the earth; that is, faith in Christ lay in the hearts of those who dwell on earth. 13. Thus, during these three days and nights souls possess both the precepts of the law and cries of repentance, so that they may be able to rise with Christ. 14. For the day and night of concealed sins, the law is general: "What you do not want to happen to you, do not do to another" [Tob 4:16; Matt 7:12; Luke 6:31]. And the cry of its repentance is: "May you not remember the sins of my youth and ignorance" [Ps 24:7]. 15. On the following day—the manifestation of sin—the law is: "Do not covet" [Exod 20:17]. And its cry of repentance is, "To you alone have I sinned, and I have done evil before you" [Ps 50:6]. 16. For the third day and night of the soul now buried by the habit of sin, the law is this: "Behold you have healed me, sin no more" [see John 5:14]. And its cry of repentance is: "Lord, free my soul from death" [Ps 114:4] and "You have led my soul out of the depths" [Ps 29:4]. 17. Through these three stages, as if there were three days, the souls rise with Christ, about whom it is said through the prophet: "The dead will rise, and those in the tombs will be called, and all on earth will shout for joy" [Isa 26:19]. 18. And about them it is said through the apostle: "Arise you who sleep and get up from the dead, and Christ will shine on you" [Eph 5:14]. And to those already rising, that is, freed from sins, he says: "If you have risen with Christ, seek those things which are above, where Christ is sitting at the right hand of God" [Col 1:1], for the Lord Jesus, risen from the dead, was taken into heaven and sits at the right hand of God the Father.

7.1. Who is this who sits at the right hand of the Father [the article to be commented on]? The human Christ. For as God he is always both with and from the Father; and so when he came to us, he did not leave the Father. For this is what it means to be God, to be everywhere whole and entire.[32] 2. Therefore, the Son is present to the Father, whole and entire in heaven, whole and entire on earth, whole and entire in the womb of the Virgin, whole and entire on the cross, whole and entire in hell, whole and entire in paradise, to which he conducted the thief [see Luke 23:43]. 3. We are not saying that he is whole and entire everywhere at different times and places, as though he is whole and entire here at one time and whole and entire elsewhere at some other time; rather we say that he is whole and entire always and everywhere.[33] 4. For if God accomplished for this light that we see with our eyes, namely, that it is whole and entire—when it is here, it is not as if it were not also in the East and in other parts of the world, but is whole and entire everywhere simultaneously, whole and entire in everything, so that it satisfies our eyes and remains undivided in itself—if created light can do this, how much more can the Creator himself do? 5. Indeed, this article of the creed, which affirms that the Son sits at the right hand of the Father, makes it clear that the very man whom Christ has assumed received the power of judging.[34]

8.1. Whence he will come to judge the living and the dead [the article to be commented on]. The book of the Acts of the Apostles [1:1-11] depicts his coming. For after he rose from the dead, he conversed with his disciples for forty days and forty nights, coming and going, eating and drinking, not because he suffered from need but to teach them the truth [about his resurrection]. 2. On the fortieth day, as the disciples were watching—their eyes, so to speak, accompanying him up—two men dressed in white stood before them and said: "Men of Galilee, why do you stand looking to heaven? The Jesus who was taken from you into heaven, this is the very one who will come just as you see him going to heaven" [1:11]. 3. He will come, my brothers, he will come, that one who previously came in a hidden way will come openly in power; the very one who was judged will come as the one to judge; the one who stood trial before men is about to judge all men. 4. "God will come in an open way" [Ps 49:3]—what does it mean to say, "God will come in an open way?" Not as before, a humble man, but as the God-man, sublime in majesty. 5. "And he will judge" [Ps 49:3-6; 95:13; 97:9]. How will he judge? Surely not as an earthly judge who will interrogate witnesses to convict you or to secure the truth by torture with the result that he punishes the person who has confessed: When that Judge, Justice Itself, takes the judgment seat, the evil conscience is witness against itself. 6. This Judge, beloved, is not hindered by grace nor overcome by mercy nor bought by money nor appeased by apology. But here, here while there is still time, here let the soul do whatever it can for itself, where the place of mercy is. 7. But there at the moment of judgment whatever a soul can do for itself will not stand the test, for it is a place of justice only. Here let the soul do penance in order to change the sentence; here let the soul give bread, in order later to get salvation; here let it act mercifully, in order there to find forgiveness.

9.1. We believe in the Holy Spirit [the article about to be commented on]. We affirm that the Holy Spirit is God, certainly not that the Father and the Son and the Holy Spirit are three Gods, but one; for one is [their] eternity, one is [their] majesty, one is [their] power.[35] 2. The Father is not the Son, but the Father is Father of the Son; the Son is not the Father, but is the Son of the Father; the Holy Spirit is neither the Father nor the Son, but the Spirit is of the Father and of the Son: three persons but one God.[36] 3. "Why," you ask, "do you say three names and one God? Show how this can be understood by either reason or some illustrative example." What reason or what example can be used to illustrate this unseen reality? 4. Indeed, may his Majesty indulge us, for our weakness has fashioned a certain analogy drawn from his creation by which Your Charity might understand—indeed, unless he permitted it, who among us would dare speak of his divinity? 5. It is not meaningless that, since every creature is subject to the Creator, our God chose to appear in no other form than fire. For he appeared to Moses in the burning bush [Exod 3:2], and he led the sons of Israel in a column of fire [Exod 13:21], and he poured out the gift of the Holy Spirit on his assembled disciples in tongues of fire [Acts 2:3]. 6. For this element of fire holds a great mystery that can stir up the curiosity of the inquirer. Behold in the fire we see three things: the flame, its brilliance, and its heat; yet, though there are three, there is one light. 7. They flame up at one and the same time, yet they remain together. The fire does not precede its radiance, nor the radiance, the heat. And they are one without disunity and three without confusion; although they are one, they are three. 8. They work together, and, although they work without separation, the flame is one thing, the radiance another, and the heat still another. 9. For when it comes to the flame burning, there both the radiance and heat are at work; when it comes to the radiance shining, the flame and heat work simultaneously; and when it comes to the heat heating, flame, heat, and radiance act together. 10. Thus, when it is asserted that God made the world, the understanding is [this], the Father in and through the Son and with the Holy Spirit. And when we say that the Son suffered for us, we understand the suffering of the Son to have been accomplished by the Father and the Son and the Holy Spirit.[37] 11. And when the remission of sins is attributed to the Holy Spirit, we understand that the entire Trinity without distinction also gives the gift. 12. These things are said to Your Charity on account of the Arian heretics as well as others who have opinions about God other than is worthy.[38] As for the rest that could be said, it is beyond expression and comprehension, nor can it be explained by the words of angels; how much the more impossible for the words of humans!

10.1. [We believe] in the remission of sins. Holy baptism completely destroys all sins, both original and personal: things said, things done, things thought, things known, things forgotten—all are discharged. 2. He who created the person makes him anew; he who is one that does not look for merit remits sins: for grace precedes even this second infancy, so that, liberated through Christ, those who were once captives in Adam and bound by the devil are free.[39]

11.1. [We believe] in the resurrection of the flesh [the article about to be commented on]. That we will be raised—this is the entire hope of our faith. "Indeed all will rise," says the Apostle, "but we will not all be changed" [1 Cor 15:51]. 2. The good will rise; the evil will rise: but the good, to enjoy eternal blessedness; the evil, to be punished by everlasting fire. At that point the faithful will be separated from the unfaithful, so that faith may receive its reward, and faithlessness obtain its place of punishment. 3. Let unbelievers not deceive themselves vainly when they hear the words of the psalm: "The wicked will not rise in judgment" [Ps 1:5]. "In judgment," it says; that is, they will not rise to be judged, because already they have been condemned because of their faithlessness in the past, according to the dominical teaching: "He who does not believe has already been judged" [John 3:18]. 4. Moreover, in order to remove all doubt from the hearts of unbelievers, the Apostle used the simile of the sower of seed: "Fool, the seed you sow does not come to life unless it dies" [1 Cor 15:36]. 5. Indeed, about what happens in a seed, I think none of you are ignorant: how grain, once ground, cleaned, and stored, is produced, spread, and planted.[40] In fact, were the fertility of the harvest not assured, these preparations would be considered senseless. 6. Even so, when the seeds are planted and disappear from sight, they lie under the soil. Indeed, if curiosity were to require one to inspect them before the rains come, it would reveal the rotting and disintegration of what had been planted whole. And if hope for the harvest is abandoned, the heavy-hearted farmer puts the crop to the torch, for he is convinced that what he had stored up was lost. 7. Moreover, when the rains have come, does he not take delight in watching the wheat budding, the stem coming up, the node arriving, the stalk lengthening, the ear coming out?

Indeed, does he not take delight in seeing that what was lying dead has thus come back to life! 8. Yet the earth cannot credit itself with fertility, because, "the Lord gives the sweetness" [Ps 84:13]. For if the rains do not fall from above, the earth will not yield good ears; rather it yields ears that are thrown into the fire instead of being stored in the granary. 9. So it is with our earth, that is, our flesh, whether here [on earth] or there [at the resurrection]. Let it not claim any merit for itself. Instead let it realize that it is about to exchange grace in this life for grace in eternal life.

12.1. That we will be raised, that we will be delivered from sin— that complete good will last forever, and so, [that total] good will be everlasting, because it will last in eternal life. 2. But what is that good which God promises to his saints? Who will explain his words? Indeed, it is easier for us to say what eternal life is not than what it is. 3. Death is not there, nor is mourning there, nor is weariness there, nor is sickness, nor is hunger; no thirst, no heat, no deterioration, no want, no sorrow, no sadness. 4. Note, we have said what is not there, but do you want to know what is? "Neither has the eye seen this, nor ear heard, nor has it occurred to the human heart what God has prepared for those who love him" (1 Cor 2:9; Isa 64:4). But if [what is there] has not arisen in the human heart, then let the human heart rise to it. 5. Let the heart be cleansed from every impurity, so that it can carry God about, the true and eternal justice. For God dwells in the heart of the believer, and of the one who takes delight in him; for, indeed, man dwells in God, that is, in eternal life, which is the reward for loving God.

6. The person who is not in the church of God is able neither to love nor to hold him dear; for everyone outside it is not with God, who is eternal life.[41] 7. The last part of this mystery [of the creed] is completed through the church—that mother fertile, virginal, and chaste, spread abroad everywhere, who bears spiritual children for God, who nourishes infants spiritually with the milk of his words, 8. who teaches little children wisdom, who guards with her chastity adolescents against unbridled excess and impurity, who arms young men with the strength of virtue against the devil, who teaches the old prudence, and who makes the more advanced in age venerable. 9. Through her, young men and women, the old along with the young, every age group, and both sexes praise the name of the Lord. She recalls the wandering children, deeply laments the dead, and

feeds with himself those who persevere without fail.[42] 10. This church, beloved, let us love; may all of us cleave inseparably to such a mother, so loving, so caring, so mindful. With and through her thus may we deserve to be perpetually united to God the Father. Amen.

THE THIRD HOMILY ON THE CREED

INTRODUCTION

1.1. Holy Mother the Church, who bore your brothers and sisters with the highest spiritual joy, has conceived you in the womb through this most holy sign of the cross;[1] how long will it be, new offspring of such a future mother, before she restores you, reborn through the washing, to the true light, feeds those whom she carries in her womb with proper food, and joyfully conducts you, rejoicing, to the day of birth? 2. She is not bound by the sentence of that Eve who bore children in sorrow and groaning, who themselves were weeping rather than rejoicing [Gen 3:16]. She undid what Eve has done, so that the offspring the latter brought to death through disobedience the former restored to life through obedience.[2]

THE PIVOTAL RITES

3. All the rites that were and are enacted among you through the ministry of God's servants by exorcism, prayers, spiritual songs, insufflations, the goatskin, bowed necks, bare feet—this trembling endured for the gift of full peace of mind—all these things, I say, are food which nourishes you in the womb, so that your joyful mother may show you, reborn from baptism, to Christ.[3] 4. You have received also the creed: protection against the poison of the serpent for those in the process of birth.[4] In the Apocalypse of the apostle John [12:1–4] it is written that the dragon stood in full view of the woman about to give birth, in order that when she gave birth, he would eat the child born [of her].[5] 5. Let none of you ignore [the fact] that the dragon is the devil; know that the virgin signifies Mary, the chaste one, who gave birth to our chaste head. 6. She also embodied in herself a figure of the holy church: namely, how, while bearing a son,

67

she remained a virgin, so that the church throughout time bears her members, yet she does not lose her virginity.[6] 7. With God's help we are about to explain the sentences of the most holy creed, that we may impress deeply on your understanding the content of each [article]. Your hearts are prepared because your enemy has been driven from them [by exorcism]. 8. The house has been cleaned, may no vanity remain; lest he who abandoned it, when he enters, bring back with him seven worse than he, and the last state of this man, as the gospel says, will be made worse than the first [Luke 11:24–26]. 9. As soon as the worst of all attackers shall have been driven out, the best of all masters is brought in. Who is the attacker? The devil. What does he invade? Man, whom he did not make and, in fact, deceived. 10. He promised immortality and pledged him [to a life of] sin.[7] You have professed to renounce him. In your profession, recorded by God and his angels, you said: "I renounce." Renounce not only with [your] voices but also with conduct; not only with the sound of the tongue but also in living act; not only by the sounds of your lips but by the public declaration of words. 12. Know that you have enlisted in a struggle with the slippery, ancient, and begrimed enemy. Let him find none of his works in you after renunciation, lest by right, then, he draw you back into servitude. 13. Christian, may you realize and admit when you do one thing and profess another: faithful in name, showing in action something other than holding true to the commitment of your faith. You enter the church for a little to pour out prayers, yet in a short time you can be seen shouting shamelessly in the theatrical spectacles.[8] 14. What do the pomps of the devil, which you have renounced, mean to you? Why do you limp along as if you had a pair of swollen testicles? If God is your master, go after him; if the world, go after it [1 Kgs 18:21]. 15. If God is chosen, let him be served according to his will; if the world is chosen, why does the heart pretend accommodation to God? 16. Whoever among you chooses the world after despising God, the world itself abandons. You do not choose to fulfill the will of God as a good person, so the will of God is fulfilled in you as evil. You can follow the [diabolic] fugitive up to this point; if you can catch him, hold on to him. 17. Oh, I see, you are fooling yourself; you cannot. For he, while hurrying along in his smooth-flowing motion like a torrent, sees you clinging to and holding him; he grasps you, not to save but to ruin you. 18. What do the pomps of the devil mean to you, lover of Christ? Do not fool yourself: for God hates such people, nor does he count for his own those whom he sifts out as deserters from his way [see Luke 22:31]. 19. Behold, how the world is in ruins; behold, how God has filled the world with such great misfortunes; behold, how bitter the world is, and yet it is loved! What would we do if it were sweet? 20. O wicked world, perjuring yourself before the weak; what would you do were you to last? If you were sweet, whom would you not deceive? If you were bitter, what food would you not spoil? 21. Beloved, do you choose to reject [such] a world? Choose to love the Creator of the world, and believe, renouncing worldly pomps, whose leader is the devil with his angels.

THE CREED

2.1. Believe in such a way that you may desire to see what you believe. Someone says, "Lo, I believe and desire to see what I believe; would that it be revealed to me that my faith might delight in this vision!" 2. If you were to see now, you would not believe; therefore, you believe because you do not see. So believe that you may see. Faith is work; vision is God's reward. You want first to receive the reward, when you have not yet undertaken the drudgery of work. 3. Is it not the case that for everyone under your supervision the reward is not given unless the work is completed? What you expect of your servant, expect this from your Lord. 4. Through faith he confers on you what he trains you for. By deferring vision of him, he commends rather than denies his gift, so that you will more amply desire the gift deferred, lest you undervalue the gift too quickly given. 5. Nonetheless, he who beneficently withholds his vision now, will not desert you. Your eyes do not see him, yet he attends to you all the time. Summon the eyes of faith. 6. Do you not look upon his face when you believe in his only begotten Son? Do you not see his hands when you consider every creature? Do you not hear his mouth, when you listen as his commandments are recited? 7. How can you pour out your prayer unless you know that you reach him, concerning whom the prophet says: "Behold the eyes of the Lord are on the just, and his ears are open to their prayers" [Ps 33:16].[9] 8. If, however, you also seek to recognize his feet, listen to those who wish to be his feet: "How beautiful are the feet of those who proclaim peace, who proclaim the good tidings" [Isa 52:7]? 9. We have been circumscribed by [our] members; but God is not restricted to these human members, because he is not in place but is everywhere entire.[10] 10. We speak according to the dictates of human understanding, not according to the inexplicable power of divine majesty. 11. Do you want to know what [divine majesty] is? Consider the creature and understand the creator; study what he made, and you will understand him who created all things. 12. Behold, the prophet says to God: "The highest heavens do not grasp you" [2 Chr 6:18].[11] And he whom the heavenly spaces do not grasp, the narrow limits of the human heart grasp, since he himself says, "I will walk among them and I will dwell with them" [see 2 Cor 6:16].[12] 13. And the Lord himself [says]: "He who loves me will be loved by my Father; and I will love him, and I and my Father will come to him and we will make our dwelling with him" [John 14:21, 23]. 14. Behold what kind of being made you—the Almighty, who created you. First acknowledge who you are, and [then] you will know who made you who you are. 15. An earthly king, thus, is mortal, because he is visible. The heavenly King is immortal and, therefore, invisible. An earthly king, although he creates nothing, nonetheless holds all things in his power; do you not believe that the king, who created everything, governs and rules the whole of it? 16. "In what way," you ask, "does he rule the whole of it? After all, there is so much evil in the world, and he does not accept responsibility for it!" O human, do you, then, deny his power, because he shows such patience? 17. Indeed, he does not send the sinner away unpunished. He takes care of him either with correction through penitence or with punishment at the final judgment. 18. Whoever you are who asks about evil, hear me, because all of us are evil. If, as you wish it, God were immediately to punish evil with evil, no one would be left to murmur about anyone! 19. But this great King, therefore, who knew how to rule what he created, does not fulfill perverse desires, but exercises his control, in order to teach you his patience. 20. Surely you do not want to change God by your madness: He who made you rules you; for if you wished to be ruled by yourself, you, on your own, would immediately fall. The first man stood as long as he clung to God: he abandoned [God], and he was abandoned. 21. He wished to prove his power, and he found misery, both ours and his own. How good it would have been for him had he done what the psalm admonished: "Cast onto the Lord your cares, and he will nourish you" [Ps 54:23]. If that man, then, did not want to be on his guard, let people be wary or [at least] be taught by experience.

22. Let us confess, let us understand that we have a King immortal and invisible, "Whom no one has seen or is able to see with his eyes" [1 Tim 6:16]. These are the words of the Apostle.

3.1. If no human has seen [him], how did he speak with Moses face to face, as if one were talking to one's friend? The question is asked too little. 2. For the Lord says, "Even as I speak with others in riddles, so I will speak with Moses as my servant; I will speak with him face to face" (Exod 33:11).[13] 3. And the scripture adds what I said above, "Because Moses was speaking with God face to face, just as someone speaks to his friend" [Num 12:7–8; see Exod 33:11]. 4. If he were speaking with him face to face, he was seeing him; [then] how can the apostolic saying be true, that "no one ever has seen God, nor can one see him" [1 Tim 6:16; see Exod 33:23]? 5. But if Moses saw him, how come a little later the same Moses asks the Great [King], and says, "If I have found grace before you, show me your face," and the Lord replies, "Indeed, my face will not be shown to you; for no one who sees my face lives" [Exod 33:20]? 6. Where is what he saw? And if he saw it, why did he want to see what he was seeing? Or in what way was that denied to him which had already been shown to him? 7. The mind is challenged. Moses saw God not with the eyes of the body but with those of the mind. And since this everlasting light that is God had enlightened him more than others, it was therefore said, "Face to face he was speaking with him," as if it were to have said, "More than all, it was shown to [Moses]." 8. But in this [verse] it is [also] said, "One cannot see my face and live"; it is plain that no one can see God with these eyes of the body. 9. Your Charity ought to learn what exactly was granted to God's most faithful servant, Moses, so that what he desired so much would not be frustrated in everyone else. 10. It was said to him by the Lord, just as scripture itself recounts it: "Go, climb up the mount of Horeb and stand there, and my splendor will pass before you, and you will see my hindquarters; my face, however, will not be shown to you" [Exod 33:21, 23].[14] 11. Lest an erroneous understanding by chance creep in, or a heretical sense, and someone think that God is corporeal, let pious faith and Catholic teaching be vigilant. 12. For the divine scripture speaks in mystical figures, respecting temporal realities, on which, once recalled, [scripture] shed light by means of truth made clear. The fact that Moses was commanded to ascend and stand on the rock on Mount Horeb is not devoid of mystery.[15] 13. This is the very rock that, having been struck, produced water for the thirsty people, about which holy David says, "He sundered the rock, and water flowed from it" [Ps 77:20]. 14. Moreover, the Apostle, explaining this, says, "Our fathers ate the same spiritual food and drank the same spiritual drink. For they were drinking the spiritual rock following them; the rock, however, was Christ" [1 Cor 10:3–4]. 15. Such are the hindquarters of God, the Christ of God. Moses, in prophesying, sees what Paul, in explaining, sees: "When the fullness of time came," he says, "God sent his Son made from a woman" [Gal 4:4]. 16. He uses "woman" here, following the Hebrew custom of speaking, which calls all females women. For it is written, "Separate out the women who have not yet known men [Num 31:18]; 17. and about Eve herself it says, "He made her into a woman" [Gen 2:22]; before he united her with a man, he called her a woman.

4.1. Moreover, faith and truth preach that Christ was born of a virgin [the article to be commented on]. Such [is what] you have understood; such, you have said you believe [in saying], "I believe." 2. This birth of God and man was accomplished for the sake of humankind. Proceeding from the heart of the Father, this sublime Majesty poured itself into the womb of the mother.[16] Piety made it imperative that man, found fallen, might be found restored to God the Father through a mediator. 3. Nevertheless, beloved brothers, extraordinary is this second birth. Perhaps, someone can describe that first birth by which [the Son] was born from the Father without any mother?[17] 4. If we cannot explain this [first birth], when are we going to be strong enough even to begin [to explain] that [second birth]? If the first so challenges us that it yields [only] to faith, when will we grasp that second birth, which even the hearts of the prophets were not able to comprehend? 5. Now about the second extraordinary and ineffable birth, let us say something, namely, it happened that the Word became flesh and dwelled among us [see John 1:14]. For who is not sorely afraid, when one hears that God is born? 6. You hear the one being born; see in this very birth the one who does miracles. The stomach of the virgin grows; the gateway of modesty remains closed; the uterus of the mother is filled without any embrace of a father; she who herself has no knowledge of a spouse feels her offspring. 7. An angel speaks to the virgin and her heart is prepared by the virgin;[18] Christ is conceived by faith. Are you amazed at this? Continue to be amazed. A mother and virgin bears a child, pregnant yet intact; the son, who also made the mother herself, is born without a human father. 8. The maker of all things is made among all things; the ruler of the entire world is carried by his mother's hands; he will suck the breast while ruling the stars. He is silent, yet the Word. 9. Not yet does his voice tell who he is, though all creation proclaims its Creator's birth. The angels announce it to the shepherds, the stars invite the Magi; the rusticity of the shepherds flees at the announcement of the angels; the curiosity of the Magi is answered by the language of the heavens. 10. The Magi proclaim the king of the Jews; the Jews deny it; the former seek to worship, and the latter, to kill.[19] The Magi tell King Herod that they seek a newborn king [see Matt 2:1–23]. 11. They inquire of the Jews about the Christ, from what city he will come to reign. Both proclaim, both confess, yet the Magi one way, and the Jews the other way; the [Magi], that the one found be adored, the [king], that the one seized be slain.

12. O Jews, you who bear the light of the law in your hands that you may show the way to others, and [yet] you shroud yourselves in darkness. Consider the Magi: The foremost of the Gentiles offer gifts to Christ, not only gold, frankincense, and myrrh, but even their own souls. 13. Yet your own iniquity repudiates you, so that, heedless of the result, you sought to kill the one who came to free you from your bonds![20] What benefit was it for you to show Herod where Christ was to be born? 14. Rather than inflicting any harm on Christ, you have injured yourselves, have you not? For, on hearing from you where the infant Christ could be found, Herod immediately commanded your people's infants to be killed. 15. Herod fell into a rage, in order to destroy the one among many, and in killing many he made himself responsible [for all their deaths]—and he did not kill the God-man whom he sought. 16. O Herod, how great is your sin! You both kill the infants and heap up the witnesses of your wickedness. And Christ was not found by you, because his hour for

suffering had not yet come. 17. Indeed, you became the persecutor of the youthful Christ and guilty of his death without doing anything to him. Nonetheless, while attempting many things against him, you have lost your very self. 18. What do you have to fear from such a king, who came to rule in such a way that he does not wish to dethrone you? The one whom you seek is the King of Kings. If you wished to obtain your kingdom you should have petitioned that you might receive your eternal kingdom from him.

19. Let Christ rule in the way that he came to rule; let him embrace believers, scoff at persecutors, stand beside those struggling, help those who labor, crown the victorious; let him give sanctity, love chastity, reward virginity. 20. Rejoice, holy virgins,[21] a virgin has given birth to Christ. You whose great faith is fruitful, do not let sterility cast you into gloom; nor ought you to be sad because you are not mothers; remaining virgins, you have begotten spiritually; you carry sons; you have not lost your integrity. 21. You have received from him the name of mother, and thus the honor of chastity remains in you forever. Love what you are, protect what you have accepted.

22. O faithful, imitate the mother of your Head, of your Spouse. He who was born of the virgin Mary has not denied you the pledge [of children]. Because he united with such a mother and in her flesh saved, the virgin mother also gave you this: the holy flesh of Christ undefiled by any contagion. 23. Nor was this flesh of his sterile. While preaching, he brought spiritual sons to life through it, and after the passion, though dead through crucifixion, [this flesh] was fertile throughout the entire world.

5.1. With full freedom rooted in this fact, let the Christian soul have confidence. For it ought not to be ashamed that it believed Christ himself to have been crucified [the article to be commented on]. 2. For that cross is not a disgrace for the faithful, but a triumph. That cross is our battle flag against our adversary the devil.[22] 3. The diabolic adversary spread terror by threatening death, but Christ promised eternal life. The adversary, the devil, was saying that the flesh would be annihilated by him. 4. To teach how his army would conquer, however, our King showed in himself that bodily death ought not to be feared. As leader, he deigned to die for all, lest the army be killed in its spirit by the devil. 5. The devil was acting in this struggle as if he were plotting against himself: He wanted perdition of souls and promised salvation to bodies. Christ was teaching the body to die [here] in time and the soul and body to live for eternity. 6. [The devil] was saying: "If you will side with me, I will give you this temporal life"; Christ was saying, "If you have not deserted me, you will not lose temporal life, and you will receive eternal life." 7. The devil was saying, "Do not choose to lose this light"; Christ was saying: "I, who made light itself, will give you a better light." 8. "What that one promises," says our Christ, "he does not have the power to give, and this light is mine, and this life was created by me; for this life, which I came to teach, is far better and more excellent." 9. Advance from good to better, lest you remain behind in a worse state by siding with the devil. In such a great struggle, while the devil takes captives, Christ frees them; the devil ensnares, Christ rescues; the devil kills, Christ revives. 10. In the heat of the contest, the adversary, the devil, thought he was killing our very King himself in the flesh, as though, with the King's head bowed, he might more easily subjugate [the King's] other members to himself. Yet mistaken in what he saw, he thought that God lay circumscribed in the smallest bit of flesh. 11. He was ignorant of so great a mystery; for [Christ] was the Mediator, and, as a result, he mingled God in man, that he might join man to God.[23] 12. The devil kills him [the Mediator], thinking him to be a strongman defending humans, and [that] he saw God liberating [from his captivity] all the humans he had created. Finally, in this passion see the spectacle of such a struggle.[24] 13. Judas is armed, that he may sell his master for a reward; he who was numbered among the disciples, becomes a participant in the plan of the Jews,[25] and he gives a feigned kiss, [contained] in which was the sign of wickedness. 14. The Jews are stirred up; they come with their torches, lanterns, and weapons. The many seek the one, and the sons of darkness come, bearing in their hands light, through which they would reveal the true light to others, the true light which they themselves, blinded, were not able to hold in their heart. 15. However, the Lord "Jesus, knowing everything that would happen to him" (for he who had come for this was not ignorant of anything), "went out to them, and said to them: 'Whom do you seek?' And they said: 'Jesus of Nazareth.' He said to them: 'I am he.' But when he said to them,

'I am he,' they drew back and fell to the ground" [John18:4–6].[26] 16. Behold the true Light, who lies hidden here under the cloud of flesh, looks at the darkness, and it fell to the ground. How then will the Jews dare to look at this brilliance, when they were so little able to stand this weakness? 17. In order that the Light might accomplish what it came for, however, the darkness gets back up. He gives [the darkness] power over himself; darkness seizes the Light, not to follow but to kill it. The Light permits himself to be seized by darkness, to be led away, to be hung, to be killed, in order that, stripped of the cloud of flesh, he might restore the splendor of his majesty. 18. But exactly what things are done in this contest? How much stronger do the servants of the devil seem than [Christ] as they grind their teeth, as they rage, as they wag their heads, as they inflict the crown of thorns, as they tear his robe, as they look on him whom they watched doing miracles, as they give him gall and vinegar, as they pierce him with a lance? 19. What kind of statement were those making, as if [proof] of their victory? "If you are the Son of God, come down from the cross" [Matt 27:40]. But he who wanted to snatch away Christ's patience was shouting this through the Jews, so that, angered by their insults, Christ might show his power but lose his patience. 20. Moreover, that strong King, and the unique plan through which he was born and through whom the whole saving plan is directed, faced down the one battle line and preserved the other through patience and power; and what he preserved, he displayed. 21. For he both preserved patience, since he did not descend from the cross, and demonstrated power, because he rose from the tomb. While he hung on the cross, the victory of the Jews [was shown to be] false; when he rose from the tomb, the true confusion of the Jews and the eternal victory of the Christians [are demonstrated]. 22. As he hung on the cross, the disciples were grieved, made sad, and scattered; when he rose from the tomb, rejoicing, they gathered in one house [Acts 1:13–14].[27] As he hung on the cross, the lack of the disciples' faith is revealed; when he rose, the in-gathering of the Gentiles [is revealed]. 23. As he hung on the cross, Peter denied him out of fear; when he rose, the whole world believed out of love. This battle was waged not only then but also is waged now. It is fought, because the members of Christ struggle with the adversary pressing them hard; [the adversary's attack] is halted, for our head already sits in heaven. 24. For this reason [Christ] chose to fight: to teach you how to conquer. But if your powers are frail, call upon the Savior himself, call on the Helper himself. When he who hung on the cross for you has seen you calling on him faithfully, he will prepare both the victory here and the crown of victory in heaven.

6.1. The third day [the article about to be commented on]. The three-day death of the Lord announced through the prophets was predicted and promised and fulfilled.[28] For the prophet Hosea says: "After two days he will raise us from the dead; on the third day we will come, and we will find him as if he were made ready even before the light" [6:3],[29] showing that we will rise in him, because he deigned to take from us the flesh in which he died. 2. What I am just now saying about this figure of Jonah the prophet, the Lord himself reveals more explicitly to the Jews: "This generation is a worthless generation; it seeks a sign, and a sign will not be given it, save for the sign of Jonah the prophet. 3. For just as Jonah was in the belly of the whale for three days and three nights, so it is also necessary that the Son of Man be in the heart of the earth for three days and three nights" [Matt 12:39–40]. 4. Let us briefly review by comparing this prophetic figure [with Christ, the fulfillment].[30] Jonah was sent to the city of Nineveh to preach its end; Christ was sent by the Father to reveal to everyone the end of the world. 5. Jonah fled to Tarshish from the face of the Lord [Jonah 1:3-4]: the flight of Jonah, the rapid passage of Christ,[31] concerning which the prophet says: "He leapt up to run like a giant along the road" [Ps 18:6]. 6. The fleeing prophet climbed aboard the ship; Christ ascended the wood [of the cross], traversing the sea of this world. A great storm erupted in the sea; the great tempest of the sea [parallels] the perfidy of the Jews. 7. Lots are cast, and so the fugitive prophet is thrown into the sea; lots are cast over the garment of Christ, so that unity is prophesied for the whole world. 8. Jonah was cast from the ship into the sea; the death of Christ in the heart of the Gentiles is evoked. The prophet was received into the beast to be guarded over, not to be devoured; listen now to the voice of Christ himself [speaking] through holy David. 9. "You will not desert my soul before hell, nor will you allow your holy one to see corruption" [Ps 15:10]. Fixed in the belly of the sea beast, holy Jonah, descending into hell, prayed; Christ, descending into hell, raised the dead. 10. On the third day the prophet was delivered to the shore unhurt; on the third day Christ, rising from the tomb, was exalted above the heavens. Because of Jonah's preaching, the city [Nineveh] was saved through penance; through the preaching of Christ the holy city, Jerusalem, was redeemed.

7.1. Assumed into heaven [the article to be commented on]. "He who descended," said the Apostle, "he it is who also ascended above all the heavens, so that he could fill all things" [Eph 4:10]. Who is this who descended? The God-man. Who is it who ascended? The very same God-man. 2. Let every person recognize him, because God was made human for humans. What he took upon himself for you, he raised to heaven; the earthly body he made heavenly. 3. And since you are certain because of such a solid guarantee, you believe that you can both rise and ascend into heaven; you are secure about such a great gift. 4. Already the man assumed by Christ reigns, sitting at the right hand of the Father; and he calls, he summons, he urges that his own receive the kingdom from him. 5. Let every soul avid for his glory hurry to him, let it pursue such a king, that it may receive power from him; he will not give it a reward of money. Rather, when the avid soul has brought him full and perfect faith, it will judge even the angels.

8.1. Whence he will come [the article about to be commented on]. Who is the one expected to come and judge the dead and the living, except the very man who deigned to hang on the cross for us? The man assumed [by the Word] is expected to come. 2. In addition, according to that which is God and equal to the Father and is always present [in him], he always judges. 3. Moreover, he will come as our Redeemer in the form in which he was assumed, so that what the prophet Zachary saw of him might be fulfilled, "They will look on the one against whom they fought" [12:10].[32] 4. Thus, the Jews will see the God-man always reigning, the one whom they had despised by denying him as he was dying. He, who will come to raise the dead, will judge them to be dead in their souls. 5. For the meaning is taken in two ways: alive and dead in soul, and also alive and dead in body. According to the first meaning, he will judge those alive in soul, the believers, then the dead in soul, those having no faith at all. 6. According to the second, he will judge those alive in the body, whom his coming will have found present; he will judge those dead in the body, whom the high God will have raised. 7. Let us choose, beloved, that his coming may find us alive in soul, lest for sinning both body and soul be condemned together by this Judge. The end of the world is near; and if, as certain people think, it is not near, [at all events the time of the] last day for each of us is uncertain.[33] What does it matter, as long as we are moving toward the life of beatitude? Let us mend our ways. Let us improve while there is time, let us improve. We have every good reason to, so that we may not fear the future day of judgment.

9.1. I believe in the Holy Spirit [the article to be commented on].[34] The Holy Spirit is God, not less so than the Father and the Son, but one majesty, one power, an inseparable Trinity, indivisible sanctity, entire and everywhere at the same time: God the Father, God the Son, God the Holy Spirit, not three gods, but one triune God. 2. The Son is not separate by time from the Father, because he is the eternal Word of the Father; the Father is not greater than the Son, because the Father begot him outside of time equally divine; indeed, through [the Son] he made time. 3. The Spirit is not less than the Father and Son, since he is the love and the harmony of the Father and the Son.[35] 4. For how is the Son less than the Father, as the Arian heretic preaches, when the Apostle calls him "the power of God and the wisdom of God" [1 Cor 1:24]? 5. If the Son is the power and wisdom of the Father, he who speaks of him as less affronts God the Father, because he contends that both less wisdom and weak power reside in [the Son]. 6. Or in what way can he say that the Holy Spirit is less than the Son, since the Apostle holds that the members of Christ are the temple of the Holy Spirit? 7. "You," he says, "are the body and members of Christ" (1 Cor 12:27), and in another place, "Do you not know," he says, "that your members are a temple and that the Holy Spirit is in you?" [1 Cor 6:19]. 8. In what way is he not God who occupies the temple? Or in what way is he less than Christ, whose members constitute the temple? There are no diverse grades among [the Three], where there is one Trinity and a threefold eternity.[36] 9. For he who composes different grades himself proceeds from unity. How can you boast, O Arian, that you have the truth, when grave error, which separates you from Catholic teaching, testifies to heresy, sets you apart from the whole world, and has condemned you to a corner [of the world]?[37] 10. Brethren, beware of heretical teachings as the crafty devices of wolves. Sheep of Christ, hear the voice of your shepherd, who says: "He who enters through the door of the sheepfold, he is the shepherd. However, the one who enters in another part, he is a thief and a robber" [John 10:2, 1]. 11. Thieves, beware; robbers beware: the shepherd does not cease to cry alarm, and he does not suffer the [guard] dogs to be silent. A sheep does not separate itself from the supreme shepherd, lest the sheep expose itself to the ravages of the most wretched wolf-abductor.

10.1. For the remission of sins [an article about to be commented on]. Cling to [your belief] with strength, hope with fidelity, look forward with patience. With your old state forsaken, a new state will be given you through baptism. 2. The soul will be unburdened of its baggage of sins, so that, adorned with the freedom of a new life, the soul may, with divine help, brandish its arms with vigor against the devil. And may it so conquer him by whom it was conquered, that, brought into the kingdom of God, the soul, safe from the conquered enemy, may reign with its head, Christ.

11.1. The resurrection of the flesh [the article about to be commented on]. Great faith is necessary, because great reward is promised. Pay no attention to what happens now but to what may then be, for what happens now distresses many. 2. Who is not moved, when one sees such enchantment, such beauty, such comeliness—the human form—dissolved into dust, bones scattered, consigned to the earth.[38] 3. Christian, do not let these deter you. Humankind is begotten not destroyed. Indeed, when the soul departs, its dwelling place is broken up; after all, she, the mistress who cares for the house of clay and restores its ruins, is not at hand. 4. For the soul departs to procure the eternal kingdom as the great reward.

> Soul, what are you afraid of? You have been consecrated to Christ the Lord; and with his grace, you live properly and struggle to come to the kingdom of God. 5. So why are you afraid of the chariot of death?[39] For you have set out and your flesh suffers injury for a time. But reigning with the most heavenly King, you return, and what is given back to you is such that it cannot be corrupted and remains with you forever. 6. If you continue along on your journey, so that you end it well, do you not believe that a better lodging will be prepared for you by the one who manages the kingdom of heaven in such a superior way? 7. If this perishable, fragile world of clay has exhibited such beauty for you, will it not exhibit so much more beauty for you when restored and made heavenly? 8. If you love this world so much that remains only for a little

while and lasts for a season, how much more will you love that one, which will lack nothing in beauty, because it will remain eternally?

12.1. In the holy creed it follows that in life eternal we may secure everything we believe in and hope for. Eternal life, beloved, will never become sour, but will always grow sweeter. 2. If life is loved, why is true life not sought? For if life is loved, then that life is sought which never ends. And if it is loved, why is it not sought? Or, if sought, why—since it is not here—do [seekers] not hasten to that place where it is? 3. Why? For Life itself, although far off, came to us—Christ is "True God and eternal life" (1 John 5:20). He came to us when we were lost; once found, he redeemed us; True Life itself came here to the region of death. 4. He gave us a taste of his wisdom; we have tasted and found that it is sweet. He led the way; he invited us to follow. And so, are we afraid of that great gift, of which we have had such a taste? 5. Life came to you; recompense the exchange; you and I have come to Life. He took the vehicle of death, so that he might free you as you cross over death. Accept also your death, so that, when you have come to Life, you will receive [life] from Life that you may never die.

13.1. [I believe] in the Holy Church [the article about to be commented on]. Because the boundaries of this sacrament are established by the holy church, should anyone have been found outside them, such a one will be estranged from the members of her family. For one who does not wish to have the church for one's mother does not have God for one's Father.[40] 2. Indeed, nothing that one has believed or done, however extensive the good [of it], outside the boundary of the highest good will be efficacious.[41] Mother Church is spiritual: the church is the bride of Christ—his grace, which was once endowed with his precious blood, is now made white.[42] 3. She possesses everything that she received from her husband as a dowry. I read his matrimonial contract; I will recite it. Listen, heretics, to what was written: "It was necessary for Christ to die and to rise from the dead, and for repentance and remission of sins to be preached in his name among all the nations" [Luke 24:46–47]. 4. "All the nations" means the whole world. The church possesses everything that she received from her husband as a dowry. Whatsoever congregation lurks in the corner of any heresy, is a concubine, not a married woman.[43] 5. O Arian heresy, why do you scoff, why do you despise, why seize on so many issues of the moment? [The church] suffers injury from you—the mistress from the handmaid—you inflict much abuse on her. Although she grieves over these things, the holy Catholic bride of Christ is not particularly afraid of you. For when her Spouse has taken stock, you yourself, with your children and your handmaid, will be expelled, because the sons of the servant girl are not heirs like the freeborn [wife]. 7. Let the one, holy, and true Catholic queen be recognized, the one to whom Christ gave such sovereignty that, spreading her through out the whole world and purifying her from every stain and wrinkle, he fashioned such complete beauty for his coming.[44] Amen.

NOTES

INTRODUCTION

1. Augustine, *Haer.* (PL 42.21–50); see also *Ep.* 222–24 (CSEL 57.446–54).

2. *Victoris Vitensis historia persecutionis Africanae provinciae sub Geiserico et Hunrico regibus Wandalorum,* ed. C. Halm, Monumenta Germaniae Historica (Berlin: Weidmann, 1879), 1.15, p. 5; *Victor of Vita: History of the Vandal Persecution,* trans. John Moorhead (Liverpool: Liverpool University Press, 1992), 8. About Victor, Moorhead comments: "We may therefore believe that at the time when he wrote his history he was a priest in Carthage, perhaps not formally one of the clergy of the city, who later became a bishop, possibly of Vita, his place of origin" (p. xv). Geiseric is subject to several spellings, including Gaiseric and Genseric.

3. For what follows, see R. Braun, "Quodvultdeus," *DS* 15/2:2882–89; idem, CCL 60.v–cvi; V. Grossi, "Adversaries and Friends of Augustine," in *Patrology,* ed. A. Berardino, trans. P. Solari (Westminster: Christian Classics, 1987), 4:501–3; and most recently Michael P. McHugh, "Quodvultdeus," *ATAE* 693–94.

4. G. Morin, "Pour une future édition des opuscules de saint Quodvultdeus, évêque de carthage au Ve siècle," *Revue Bénédictine* 31 (1914): 156–62. He argues that twelve homiletic works assigned to Augustine (including the creedal homilies) point to a single author on the basis of Augustinian influences, common traits, and similar content, themes, circumstances, and style, and that author was among the first successors of Bishop Aurelius of Carthage, who died about 430. Specifically he identified the successor as Quodvultdeus. In addition, he suggested that a thirteenth work, *Liber promissionum,* was Quodvultdeus's as well.

5. Thus Notker, the Stammerer, of St. Gall (d. 912), biographer of Charlemagne and liturgical innovator: *regulam omnium divinarum scripturarum* (PL 131.1001).

6. At first Augustine adopted the millenarian view current in his early years, which divided history into six ages corresponding to the six days of creation (Adam to Noah, Abraham, David, the Babylonian captivity, Jesus, and the Parousia). About the year 400 he adopted the simpler tripar-

tite view that Quodvultdeus espouses. For discussion, see Robert Markus, "History," *ATAE* 432-34; and for the *Liber*, H. Englebert, "Un example historigraphique au Ve siècle: La conception de l'histoire chez Quodvultdeus de Carthage et ses relations avec la *Cité de Dieu*," *REAug* 37 (1991): 307-20.

7. For Braun's detailed study of the manuscript tradition of the *Liber* and his reasons for attribution, see CCL 60.vii–xxxix. He first published the *Liber* in *Livre des promesses et des prédictions de Dieu*, SC 101, 102 (Paris: Éditions du Cerf, 1964), and subsequently in CCL 60 (1976). For a recent study of the *Liber*, see Daniel Van Slyke, "Quodvultdeus of Carthage: Political Change and Apocalyptic Theology in the Fifth-Century Roman Empire" (PhD diss., Saint Louis University, 2001).

8. M. Simonetti of the University of Rome, for instance, argues for the following attributions: *De accedentibus ad gratiam* 1 and 2, *De tempore barbarico* 1, and perhaps *Adversus quinque haereses* (Augustine); *De symbolo* 1, 2, and 3, *Contra Judaeos, Paganos et Arianos*, and perhaps *De cantico novo* (unknown author); and *De ultima quarta feria*, *De cataclysmo*, and *De tempore barbarico* 2 (a different unknown author): "Studi sulla letteratura cristiana d'Africa in età vandalica," *Rencidonti del R. Istituto Lombardo de Scienze e Lettere* 83 (1950): 407-24, and *La Produzione letteraria Latina fra Romani e barbari (sec. V-Viil)*, Sussidi Patristici 3 (Rome: Augustinianum, 1986), 35-39, bibliography, 226. Braun sets out his arguments for attribution to Quodvultdeus in CCL 60.xl-cvi. They rest on the manuscript traditions and the homogeneity of ideas, manner, and style.

9. For the Roman destruction of Carthage in 146 BCE, see Serge Lancel, *Carthage: A History* (Oxford: Blackwell, 1995), 396-430. The phrase is Cato the Elder's, who insisted on the destruction of the city from the beginning of his embassy in 151 BCE. For *De temp. barb.* 1 and 2, see CCL 60.423-37.

10. For the sequence, see Braun, *DS* 15:2884; and for the presence of Capreolus, see below, *De symb.* 1.1.1 (CCL 60.305), and note.

11. On Christian initiation in North Africa, see Benedict Busch, "De initiatione christiana secundum sanctum Augustinum," *ELA* 52 (1938): 159-78 (pre-Augustine, including Ambrose), 358-483 (according to Augustine); Suzanne Poque, *Augustin d'Hippone: Sermons pour la Pâque*, SC 116 (Paris: Éditions du Cerf 1966); William Harmless, *Augustine and the Catechumenate* (Collegeville, MN: Liturgical Press, 1995); T. M. Finn, *Early Christian Baptism and the Catechumenate: Italy, North Africa, and Egypt*, MF 5 (Collegeville, MN: Liturgical Press, 1992), 111-71.

12. Thus, Augustine in *De cat. rud.* 26.50 (PL 40.344-45; CCL 46.173-74). For Quodvultdeus, see below, *De symb.* 1.1.3 (CCL 60.305) and n. 3.

13. See T. M. Finn, "Ritual and Conversion: The Case of Augustine," in *Nova et Vetera: Patristic Studies in Honor of Thomas Patrick Halton* (Washington, DC: Catholic University of America Press, 1998), 148–61.

14. For a study of conversion and ritual process that notes the forces— social, cultural, and personal—that drove the development of the catechumenate, see T. M. Finn, *From Death to Rebirth: Ritual and Conversion in Antiquity* (Mahwah, NJ: Paulist Press, 1997), esp. 137–238, which analyzes the development of the catechumenate from its early stages to the fifth century; see also Harmless, *Augustine and the Catechumenate*, 39–106, for Milan and the fourth-century West.

15. Chrysostom, *Cat. bapt.* 8.1 (A. Wenger, ed., *Huit catéchèses baptismales inédites*, SC 50 [Paris: Éditions du Cerf, 1957], 247–48); Quodvultdeus, see below *De bapt.* 3.1.1 (CCL 60.349).

16. Augustine's *De cat. rud.* (PL 40.309–48; CCL 46.121–78), which was influential in Quodvultdeus's catechetical work and the *Liber,* describes the very first stage and, in so doing, sets the tone and stages; see Joseph P. Christopher, *St. Augustine: The First Catechetical Instruction*, ACW 2 (New York: Newman Press/Paulist Press, 1946), 3–11.

17. Augustine, *Serm.* 216.1 (PL 38.1077). Thus, also *competentes*.

18. See below, *De symb.* 1.1–2.28 (CCL 60.305–7), and notes.

19. Augustine, *Serm.* 229 (PL 38.1103).

20. Augustine, *Serm.* 212.1 (PL 38.1058): the occasion was the *traditio*. For the context, sermons, and chronology in Hippo, see Harmless, *Augustine and the Catechumenate*, 274–86.

21. See *Serm.* 213 (PL 38.1060–65); in 214 (PL 38.1065) Augustine says that they have an obligation to believe the creed as summarized, to memorize it, and to profess it orally in the *redditio symboli,* which, in Carthage, was the following Saturday vigil and included the scrutiny and renunciation discussed below.

22. Augustine, *Serm.* 215.1–9 (PL 38.1060–65). Credo in Deum Patrem omnipotentem, universorum creatorem et in filium eius Dominum nostrum Jesum Christum, qui conceptus est de Spiritu sancto, natus ex virgine Maria. Crucifixus, mortuus et sepultus est sub Pontio Pilato. Tertia enim die resurrexit a mortuis, ascendit in coelum, sedet ad dexteram Dei Patris, inde venturus est judicare vivos et mortuos. Et in Spiritum sanctum, remissionem peccatorum, et resurrectionem carnis et vitam aeternam per sanctam ecclesiam catholicam.

23. See below, *De symb.* 1.1.4–8 (CCL 60.305); 2.1.1–2.3 (CCL 60.335); and 3.1.1–2.3 (CCL 60:349–51), and notes. For the goatskin, see Johannes Quasten, "Theodore of Mopsuestia on the Exorcism of the Cilicium," *HTR* 35 (1942): 209–19. For Theodore it signified humankind's fallen state. The equal and opposite vestment would be the resplendent white garment of baptism, which signified rebirth in the New Paradise. For the scrutiny at Hippo,

see Harmless, *Augustine and the Catechumenate,* 260–74. He thinks that the scrutiny at Hippo took place soon after enrollment and analyzes *Serm.* 216 to develop its feel and ferocity.

24. Busch, "De initiatione christiana," 439–40; but see also Poque, *Augustin d'Hippone,* 24–33; and Harmless, *Augustine and the Catechumenate,* 274–86.

25. See below, *De symb.* 1.1.15–2.28 (CCL 60.306–10), and notes; 2.2.1–22 (CCL 60.336–37), and notes. They discuss the spectacles in detail, but see also below under "Religious Turmoil."

26. *De symb.* 1.1.10–11 (CCL 60.306), and note.

27. Augustine describes the dramatic moment in *Conf.* 8.5 (James J. O'Donnell, ed., *Augustine: Confessions I: Introduction and Text* [Oxford: Clarendon, 1992], 90); it is the *redditio symboli* of the celebrated rhetorician and Neoplatonist philosopher-convert Marius Victorinus (c. 360). Quodvultdeus provides no clear information about when the competents professed the creed, except that it was part of the Easter vigil baptismal rite.

28. Augustine, *Conf.* 8.12.28–30 (O'Donnell, 1.101–2).

29. See Finn, "Ritual and Conversion," 148–61.

30. See below, *De symb.* 1.1.8 (CCL 60.305). The theme of social equality before the rites, especially exorcism, was widespread. See Chrysostom, *Cat. bapt.* 2.13 (Wenger, SC 50.140).

31. See below, *De symb.* 1.9–11 (CCL 60.305–6), and note.

32. See Augustine, *Serm.* 259.4 (PL 38.1199).

33. Thus Lancel, *Carthage,* 436–38; and Augustine, who says, *Punicam, id est, Afram* (*Ep.* 1.2.3; PL 35.1991). Lancel observes that Punic was an indispensable tongue of communication in the rural areas and a necessary condition for being a cleric in the Numidian villages and small towns. Clearly not all Quodvultdeus's audience spoke or understood Punic, but in such a metropolis, Punic and Berber would have echoed on the streets.

34. See Lancel, *Carthage,* 428–36; J. B. Rives, *Religion and Authority in Roman Carthage from Augustine to Constantine* (Oxford: Clarendon Press, 1995); W. H. C. Frend, *The Donatist Church: A Movement of Protest in Roman North Africa,* 2nd ed. (Oxford: Clarendon Press, 1971), 37–39, 60–68. Frend observes, however, that in African towns there was a tendency for society to be divided into a small romanized group and a considerable native group (p. 66). For a fine account of both the traditions and religion based largely on the archaeological evidence, see David Soren et al., *Carthage: From the Legends of the Aeneid to the Glorious Age of Gold* (New York: Simon & Schuster, 1991), 165–266.

35. They would have immediately understood Quodvultdeus's point about the creed as contract or "pact of fidelity."

36. Frend, *Donatist Church,* 64–65.

37. See below, *De symb.* 2.2.19–20 (CCL 60.337), for a colorful dialogue about the Mediterranean shipping world.

38. Alaric and his Goths, who scourged Italy, attempted unsuccessfully to cross into Africa in 410, and there were Gothic mercenaries who were contingents in the Roman army in Africa (the Donatists were considering an alliance). Indeed, the second wife of Count Boniface (prefect of Roman Africa), Pelagia, was an Arian Goth, much to Augustine's dismay. See Justine Davis Randers-Pehrson, *Barbarians and Romans: The Birth Struggle of Europe, A.D. 400–700* (Norman: University of Oklahoma Press, 1983), 147–48.

39. Soren, *Carthage,* 181–86, here 184.

40. See Michael Signer, "Jews and Judaism," ATAE 470–73; Paula Fredriksen, "*Excaecati Occulta Justitia Dei:* Augustine on Jews and Judaism," *JEC* 3 (1995): 320–24; Yann LeBohec, "Juifs et judaisants dans l'Afrique romaine: Remarques onomastiques," *Antiquités Africains* 17 (1981): 209–29; Rives, *Religion and Authority in Roman Carthage,* 214–23.

41. See Harry J. Leon, *The Jews of Ancient Rome,* rev. ed., with a new introduction by Carolyn Osiek (Peabody, MA: Hendrickson, 1995), 135–66.

42. Tertullian, *Adv. Jud.* 1 (CSEL 70.251).

43. Augustine, *Ep.* 12.23 (CSEL 25/1.351; tr. Fredriksen, "*Excaecati Occulta Justitia Dei,*" 317 and n. 51).

44. For a recent historical and theological study of the issues, see Jeremy Cohen, *Living Letters of the Law: Ideas of the Jew in Medieval Christianity* (Berkeley: University of California Press, 1999), 1–71 (Augustinian Foundations for Latin Christian anti-Judaism); Fredriksen, "*Excaecati Occulta Justitia Dei,*" 299–324. For the East, see N. R. M. De Lange, *Origen and the Jews: Studies in Jewish-Christian Relations in Third-Century Palestine* (Cambridge: Cambridge University Press, 1976), 75–116; Robert L. Wilken, *John Chrysostom and the Jews: Rhetoric and Reality in the Later Fourth Century* (Berkeley: University of California Press, 1983), 66–94; and idem, *Judaism and the Early Christian Mind: A Study of Cyril of Alexandria's Exegesis and Theology* (New Haven: Yale University Press, 1971), 9–54. For Judaism and Christianity in North Africa, see Signer, "Jews and Judaism," 470–74.

45. Quodvultdeus, *Ad quin. haer.* 1.8 (CCL 60.262).

46. Quodvultdeus, *De symb.* 3.4.12 (CCL 60.355).

47. Quodvultdeus, *De symb.* 1.5.13–16 (CCL 60.318–19).

48. Quodvultdeus, *De symb.* 1.6.7–9 (CCL 60.321).

49. For the Jews of the homilies, see below, *De symb.* 1.5.10–19; 1.6.7–20 (CCL 60.318–19, 320–22); 2.4.1–27; 2.5.1–19 (CCL 60.338–39, 341–42); 3.4.10–19; 3.5.13–24 (CCL 60.354–55, 357–358).

50. Cohen, *Living Letters of the Law,* 1–18 (for the pre-Augustinian period) and 19–65 (Augustinian doctrine of witness).

51. Wilken, *Judaism and the Early Christian Mind,* 27. His direct concern is with fifth-century Alexandria and Cyril of Alexandria, but see his *John*

Chrysostom and the Jews, where he concentrates on the Jews of late-fourth-century Antioch and what he calls the "rhetoric of abuse."

52. Augustine, *Serm.* 62.12 (PL 38.423); and Frend, *Donatist Church,* 247-50. For a discussion of heresy and the Theodotian code, see William K. Boyd, *The Ethics of the Theodotian Code* (1906; repr., New York: AMS Press, 1969), 33-70; David Hunt, "Christianizing the Roman Empire," in *The Theodosian Code,* ed. Jill Harries and Ian Wood (Ithaca, NY: Cornell University Press, 1993), 143-58.

53. See Augustine, *Serm.* 62.12.18 (PL 38.423); and Frend, *Donatist Church,* 87, 227-43, 269, 303. The Jews were proscribed along with Donatists and Arians in 535.

54. See, e.g., Lancel, *Carthage,* 193-256 (for the religious culture of ancient Carthage); Rives, *Religion and Authority in Roman Carthage,* whose study has as part of its goal to construct a relatively clear picture of the religious life of Carthage.

55. See below, *De symb.* 2.2.5-6 (CCL 60.335-36). Rocks, mountains, caves, and springs were frequently places of sanctity for the Berbers, whose roots go back into the Stone Age, which explains some of the megalithic characteristics of their religion. See Norman A. Stillman, "Berber Religion," *ER* 2:109-11; and Marita Gimbutas, J. Stephen Lansing, "Megalithic Religion," *ER* 9:336-46. The difficulty in studying megalithic survivals is *interpretatio romana.* One current was the North African attempt to interpret their indigenous religions in Roman religious terms; the other was the attempt to assimilate Roman religion. In any case, the collections at the Bardo Museum in Tunis provide valuable illustrative Libyan and Berber evidence of material culture reflecting both currents. See M'hamed Fantar, *Le Bardo: Un palais, un musée* (Tunis: Alif, n.d.).

56. Quodvultdeus, *De symb.* 2.2.19-20 (CCL 60.337). The point about the ship's keel is particularly relevant, because it is the Phoenicians who perfected the keel ship (Soren, *Carthage,* 27). About the fish, a famous Carthaginian product was *garum,* a fish sauce made by reducing dried fish and shellfish to a powder, marinating them in a salty solution mixed with herbs (Soren, *Carthage,* 177). It was used all over the Mediterranean, assuring the kind of nourishment for which fish and seafood are still prized.

57. Quodvultdeus, *De symb.* 2.3.4 (CCL 60.337). For a discussion of religion in pre-Roman Carthage, see Lancel, *Carthage,* 193-257; and for Roman Carthage, Lancel, *Carthage,* 428-36; Rives, *Religion and Authority in Carthage,* 17-99.

58. For what follows, see Lancel, *Carthage,* 193-256 (Punic) and 428-36 (Roman survivals); Rives, *Religion and Authority in Carthage,* 173-249; Soren, *Carthage,* 235-52.

59. For an account of the excavations and interpretation, see Lancel, *Carthage,* 227-56.

60. As Juno, she symbolized femininity as mother; as Caelestis, virgin (Rives, *Religion and Authority in Carthage*, 188–90).

61. For the rise of Caelestis, see Rives, *Religion and Authority in Carthage*, 65–71.

62. See below, *De symb.* 1.5.1–279 (CCL 60.317–20).

63. Quodvultdeus, *Lib. prom.* 3.44 (CCL 60.185): Namquae cum sanctae Paschae sollemnis agseretur festivitas, collecta illic et undique omni curiositate etian adveniens multitudo, sacerdotum multorum pater et dignae memoriae nominandus antistes Aurelius, caelistis iam patriae ciuis, cathedram illic posuit in loco Caelestis et sedit ... Arelius pontifex dedicavit. Hunc legentes populi mirabantur praesago tunc spiritu acta quae praecius Dei ordo certo isto fine concluserat.

64. See below, *De symb.* 1.1.5–2.28 (CCL 60.336–37). For recent studies, see Paul Plass, *The Game of Death in Ancient Rome: Arena Sport and Political Suicide* (Madison: University of Wisconsin Press, 1995), 15–77 (gladiatorial combat); Richard C. Beacham, *The Roman Theatre and Its Audience* (Cambridge, MA: Harvard University Press, 1992), 178–91 (staging in the theater); Roland Auguet, *Cruelty and Civilization: The Roman Games* (London: George Allen & Unwin, 1972), 81–148 (hunts and chariot races). For the spectacles in their Carthaginian and Roman North African setting, see Soren, *Carthage*, 197–210; much of the contemporary sense is supplied by the mosaics recovered, for which see Soren, *Carthage*, 219–28.

65. In the West, the pillaring of the spectacles is a solid tradition already in Tertullian: he devoted the better part of his *De spectaculis* 5–15 (CSEL 20.6–16) to their indictment. The attack was no different in the East, for which see T. M. Finn, *The Liturgy of Baptism in the Baptismal Instructions of St. John Chrysostom*, SCA 15 (Washington, DC: Catholic University of America Press, 1967), 99–102.

66. Augustine, *Conf.* 6.7.11 (O'Donnell 1.64).

67. Augustine, *Conf.* 6.8.13 (O'Donnell 1.65); tr. Henry Chadwick, *Saint Augustine: Confessions* (Oxford: Oxford University Press, 1991), 101.

68. See below, *De symb.* 2.1.5 (CCL 60.334). His image actually is of the magistrate who, when he formally passes judgment, is often blinded by the smoke from the ceremonial brazier burning before him, forgetting that he too is human.

69. A Carthage plate cited in Soren, *Carthage*, 232; see also John H. Humphrey, *Roman Circuses: Arenas for Chariot Racing* (Berkeley: University of California Press, 1985), 305–6.

70. This is a précis of *De symb.* 2.2.1–10 (CCL 60.335–36). On the chariot races, see Auguet, *Cruelty and Civilization*, 120–48.

71. For the theater at Carthage, see Soren, *Carthage*, 221–24. The mime performance often took its subject from daily life and presented it as farce, including gesture, dance, music, and voice; it favored the lewd. The

pantomime aimed at a more cultured audience and featured dance, chorus, and music. The pantomimes gave stylized interpretations of both history and religious subjects. For what follows about the audience and the staging, see Beacham, *Roman Theatre*, 154–98, 180–82, especially for the "contrivances" Quodvultdeus mentions.

72. See *De symb.* 1.2.10–22 (CCL 60.308–9). Quodvultdeus contrasts the theatrical spectacles in Carthage's theater with the evangelical spectacles in the church.

73. Quodvultdeus, *De symb.* 2.2.23–27 (CCL 60.309). Auguet considers the hunts in *Cruelty and Civilization*, 81–106. Africa was tailor-made for people who liked hunting. Animals were plentiful and the hunts summoned fascination and induced extravagance. Soren focuses on a mosaic recovered from Althiburos, some 140 miles southwest of Tunis (*Carthage*, 225–28). In addition, on Byrsa Hill, where the patricians lived, there are hunting mosaics in sites among the villas.

74. See Humphrey, *Roman Circuses*, 303–5. For the circus excavations, see Naiomi Norman, "Excavations in the Circus at Carthage," *Archaeology* 40 (1987): 46–57. It was the largest structure in the whole of Roman Africa.

75. See below, *De symb.* 1.12.9–10 (CCL 60.334).

76. W. H. C. Frend notes that the story of Donatism in Roman Africa closed on a note of defiance. Citing Augustine's *Ep.* 185.1 (CSEL 57.1–2), he notes that some took steps toward separation from the empire, regarded Goths favorably, and considered common ground with the Arians (Frend, *Donatist Church*, 297).

77. For the complex history of Arianism from the standpoint of modern scholarship, see Thomas A. Kopecek, *A History of Neo-Arianism*, 2 vols., Patristic Monograph Series 8 (Cambridge, MA: Philadelphia Patristic Foundation, 1979); R. P. C. Hanson, *The Search for the Christian Doctrine of God: The Arian Controversy 318–381* (Edinburgh: T. & T. Clark, 1988); see also *Arianism after Arius: Essays on the Development of the Fourth Century Trinitarian Conflicts*, ed. Michel R. Barnes and Daniel H. Williams (Edinburgh: T. & T. Clark, 1993), esp. 3–62; Lewis Ayers, "'Remember That You Are Catholic' (serm. 52.2): Augustine on the Unity of the Triune God," *JEC* 8 (2000): 39–82, esp. 55–82, for Augustine's maturing theology of the Trinity and inseparability.

78. *De symb.* 1 presents Quodvultdeus's most extensive treatment of his *Arriani:* 1.3.9–4.38 (CCL 60.311–17) (Father and Son primarily); 1.9.1–30 (CCL 60.326–29) (the Holy Spirit); 1.13.3–13 (CCL 60.333–34) (Arian practices). In *De symb.* 2.9.12 (CCL 60.346), while concluding the article on the Holy Spirit, he simply says: "These things are said to Your Charity on account of the Arian heretics as well as others who have opinions about God other than is worthy" (CCL 60.346). In *De symb.* 3.9.4 (CCL 60.360), he says that they preach the Son as less than the Father, and in 3.13.3–5 (CCL 60.363), he

speaks of them as outside the church: Rather than *matronae-mater ecclesia,* they comprise *concubina,* who inflicts on mother church injury and contempt.

79. Quodvultdeus, *De symb.* 1.9.6 (CCL 60.326), but see also 1.3.10 (CCL 60.311).

80. The fully articulated position must be identified largely from Quodvultdeus's refutation, which extends from *De symb.* 1.3.1–4.38 (CCL 60.310–17).

81. Quodvultdeus, *De symb.* 1.4.34 (CCL 60.316). For a discussion of this emphasis in Arianism after Arius, see Rowan Williams, "Baptism and the Arian Controversy," in *Arianism after Arius,* ed. Barnes and Williams, 167–70.

82. Quodvultdeus, *De symb.* 1.9.6-7 (CCL 60.326–27).

83. Augustine, *Trin.* 2.5.7 (PL 42.848–49; CCL 50.87–89).

84. Augustine, *Trin.* 5.2.3 (PL 42.912; CCL 50.207–8): Est tamen sine dubitatione substantia, vel si melius hoc apellatur, essentia, quam Graeci ousian vocant. Quodvultdeus, *De symb.* 1.9.18 (CCL 60.328): Sed adhuc vanas tuas machinas diversasque comparationes de Patris et Filii et Spiritus sancti substantia, catholica doctrina suffodiat. See also 1.9.27 (CCL 60.329): divina illa substantia manens in se ipsa sicuti est.

85. Augustine, *Trin.* 5.1.2 (PL 42.912; CCL 50.206–7). For a treatment of Augustine's *De trinitate,* see Rowan Williams, *"Trinitate, de,"* ATAE 845–51.

86. Timothy Barnes, "The Arians of book V, and the Genre of De Trinitate," *JTS* n.s. 44 (1993): 189–90. Ambrose details the six Arian propositions about the Son that he seeks to rebut: (1) The son is not like the Father; (2) the Son did have a beginning in time; (3) the Son was created; (4) the Son was not good; (5) the Son is not the true Son of God, nor omnipotent; (6) the Son is not one with the divinity of the Father (*De fid.* 1.5.34–40) (PL 16.536).

87. Barnes, "Arius, Arianism," *ATAE* 59–60; see also R. P. C. Hanson, "Homoian Arianism," in his *Search for the Christian Doctrine of God,* esp. 557–72.

88. Quodvultdeus, *De symb.* 1.13.5 (CCL 60.334).

89. See *De symb.* 1.13.6 (CCL 60.334), for money and compulsion; and Hanson, *Search for the Christian Doctrine of God,* 575.

90. Quodvultdeus, *De symb.* 1.13.6 (CCL 60.334).

91. See Michel Meslin, *Les Ariens d'Occident, 335-430,* Patristica Sorbonensia 8 (Paris: Éditions du Seuil, 1967), 382–90; and his "Baptism," *ER* 2:62. See also Rowan Williams, "Baptism and the Arian Controversy," in *Arianism after Arius,* ed. Barnes and Williams, 171–74.

92. Victor of Vita, *Hist. pers. Afric. prov.* 1.22 (C. Halm, ed., *Victor Vitensis,* 6; Moorhead, *Victor of Vita,* 11 [see n. 2 above]).

93. *Liber fidei catholicae* in *Victor Vitensis,* ed. Halm, 2:56–101; Moorhead, *Victor of Vita,* 44–63).

94. For the text, see n. 22 above.

95. See Quodvultdeus, *De symb.* 3.13.1–4 (CCL 60.363). In *Contra Judaeos* he writes: Apud catholicam, dilectissimi, noveritis esse tantum veram fidem, germanam pacem, perpetuam salutem. Non enim in angulo est, se ubique tota est (20.1; CCL 60.255).

96. Quodvultdeus, *De symb.* 1.6.4–5 (CCL 60.320). In *De symb.* 2.6.6–7 (CCL 60.343), he indicates that he prefers *spiritualem intellectum* for this kind of interpretation.

97. Augustine, *Doct. Chr.* 2.11.16 (PL 32.43; CCL 32.42); 2.15.22 (PL 34.46; CCL 32.47–48). For discussion, see Bruce M. Metzger, *The Early Versions of the New Testament* (Oxford: Clarendon Press, 1977), 285–330; G. W. H. Lampe, ed., *The Cambridge History of the Bible,* vol. 2, *The West from the Fathers to the Reformation* (Cambridge: Cambridge University Press, 1969), 27–35; James J. O'Donnell, "Bible," *ATAE* 99–103. For the editions, see Bonafatius Fischer, ed., *Vetus Latina: Die Reste der Altlateinischen Bible* (Freiburg: Herder, 1949–); Adolf Jülicher, ed., *Itala: Das Neue Testament in alt-lateinischer Überlieferung* (Berlin/New York: Walter de Gruyter, 1972–).

98. Thus, O'Donnell, "Bible," *ATAE* 99–103. Quodvultdeus's important variations from the Vulgate and Itala are often noted in the endnotes.

THE FIRST HOMILY ON THE CREED

1. The rites that had been celebrated in the vigil were scrutiny, the renunciation of Satan, and the profession of the creed *(redditio symboli)* discussed above in the introduction (see under "Pivotal Rites"). The vigil of the following Saturday would be the Easter vigil celebration of the baptismal rites. Quodvultdeus will now, on Sunday morning, explain the creed handed over orally the week previously in vigil also discussed in the introduction (see under *"Traditio Symboli"*), and now in the extended commentary that follows. These opening passages of the homily (1.1.1–4 [CCL 60.305]) constitute a formal rhetorical exordium in which Quodvultdeus addresses his patron *(sanctitate vestrae)* with a customary title, almost certainly Bishop Capreolus, whom he succeeded in 437, but it may be a formal salutation for the congregation, since Quodvultdeus uses the phrase elsewhere as a form of address for the congregation (see, e.g., *De symb.* 2.9.12 [CCL 60.346]).

2. The word of God and its exposition as food constituted a traditional image by Quodvultdeus's time (see the introduction under "The Creedal Homilies and the Catechumenate"). His older contemporary John Chrysostom was accustomed to calling catechetical instructions for catechumens a "spiritual banquet," and Chrysostom speaks of the "excellent teachers" as filling the hearers well with nourishment that will sustain them on their journey home (*Cat. bapt.* 8.1 [SC 50.247–48]). For commentary, see

T. M. Finn, *The Liturgy of Baptism in the Baptismal Instructions of St. John Chrysostom*, SCA 15 (Washington, DC: Catholic University of America Press, 1967), 60–65. As with his patristic predecessors, Quodvultdeus regards the creed as a normative statement of the fundamental teaching of scripture.

3. The reference is to the rite of inscription discussed in the introduction (see under "The Catechumenate"), which was already traditional in Augustine's time. For a discussion of the North African rites for the making of catechumens and for those selected for baptism (the *competentes*), see Benedict Busch, "De initiatione christiana secundum sanctum Augustinum," ELA 52 (1938): 159–78 (pre-Augustine), and 385–483 (Augustine, esp. 401–83 on the specific rites); T. M. Finn, *From Death to Rebirth: Ritual and Conversion in Antiquity* (Mahwah, NJ: Paulist Press, 1997), 212–38; William Harmless, *Augustine and the Catechumenate* (Collegeville, MN: Liturgical Press, 1995), 80. Augustine reports that inscription consisted of exorcism (insufflation coupled with an exorcismal formulary), the imposition of hands, the sign of the cross, and the ingestion of salt (*Conf.* 1.11.17 [O'Donnell 1:9]); T. M. Finn, *Early Christian Baptism and the Catechumenate: Italy, North Africa, and Egypt*, MF 5 (Collegeville, MN: Liturgical Press, 1992), 154–57. As an example of the kind of preliminary instruction that Quodvultdeus's catechumens would have had, see Augustine, *De catechizandis rudibus*, which he wrote for his clergy and their inquirers (*accedentes*). Augustine describes the normal circumstances of the rite for inquirers in *De cat. rud.* 26.50 (CCL 46.121–78; J. Christopher, ed., *St. Augustine: The First Catechetical Oration*, ACW 2 [Westminster, MD: Newman Press; Mahwah, NJ: Paulist Press, 1946], 82–83 and nn. 314–16, 145–47). For the church as mother, see Joseph C. Plumpe, *Mater Ecclesia: An Inquiry into the Concept of the Church as Mother in Early Christianity*, SCA 5 (Washington, DC: Catholic University of America Press, 1943); and for baptismal rebirth, see Walter Bedard, *The Symbolism of the Baptismal Font in Early Christian Thought*, SST n.s. 45 (Washington: Catholic University of America Press, 1951).

4. It was customary to consider the inscribed as part of the church. For Tertullian, they were "young novices [*novitioli:* military recruits] who were just beginning to hear the flow of divine discourse" (*De paenitentia* 6 [PL 1.1230]). Quodvultdeus expresses a customary way of understanding their membership: In the womb of Holy Mother Church, they were as yet unborn, but the "property" of the church much as, in the Talmud, the fetus is the property of the mother.

5. This is the earliest full description of a rite known in the West as "scrutiny." Ambrose called the rite *scrutaminum*, a unique solemn exorcism that involved a physical exam to determine whether any impurity inhered in the bodies of the competents (*Explanatio symboli* 1 [PL 17.155C]): "There was a search—lest anything unclean still cling to the body of anyone of you. Using exorcism we sought and brought about the sanctifying not only of your body,

but of your soul as well" (cited in Harmless, *Augustine and the Catechumenate,* 96). Venereal disease and other symptoms of diabolic possession may have been the point. In Augustine the usual term is *scrutinium,* for which see Busch, "De initiatione christiana," 434–38. Quodvultdeus emphasizes the rite as an exorcismal examination *(examen).* About the rite, Augustine says: "Whatever [Satan] incited by the most scandalous suggestions, whatever by the most shameful allurements now made public, will be emptied out of you" *(Serm.* 216.7.7 [PL 38.1080] tr. Finn). The pivotal rites in the liturgy of conversion, discussed in the introduction (see under "The Pivotal Rites"), were celebrated the week before Easter: (1) the scrutiny in the Saturday night vigil; (2) the renunciation of Satan, followed by (3) the profession of allegiance to Christ, that is, the profession of faith *(redditio symboli).* The works just cited for Ambrose and Augustine, coupled with this homily of Quodvultdeus are classic examples of homilies delivered on the occasion of the pivotal rites. See T. M. Finn, "It Happened One Saturday Night: Ritual and Conversion in Augustine's North Africa," *JAAR* 58 (1990): 589–616.; Suzanne Poque, *Augustin d'Hippone: Sermons pour la Pâque,* SC 116 (Paris: Éditions du Cerf, 1966), 26–33. The seminal study was that of A. Dondeyne, "La discipline des scrutins dans l'Église latine avant Charlemagne," *RHE* 28 (1932): 5–33.

6. It may have literally been goatskin, but it may well have been sackcloth or burlap. The rite originated in the East, spreading west to North Africa and Spain. For Augustine, see Busch, "De initiatione christiana," 438–40; Harmless, *Augustine and the Catechumenate,* 263. The symbolism was twofold: It reminded the competents of the wretchedness to which sin had reduced them, and it recalled the "garments of skin" with which Adam was clothed after the Fall, signifying his degradation. See Johannes Quasten, "Theodore of Mopsuestia on the Exorcism of the Cilicium," *HTR* 5 (1942): 209–19.

7. This was the psalm chanted during scrutiny in North Africa; its opening lines are, "O Lord, you have searched me and known me; you know when I sit down and when I rise up; you discern my thoughts from afar." It speaks about the darkness that envelops one, the wings of the morning, being knit together in the womb, being known in one's most secret parts, oppressed by enemies, and the discovery of any secret and wicked way in one—all themes appropriate to the scrutiny. In the course of his homily on the occasion, Augustine cites a number of psalms; as a result, it is uncertain what the psalm might have been in Hippo; clearly this was the psalm in Carthage.

8. The egalitarianism of the baptismal rites was an important theme in the East as well, especially in exorcism. Before the exorcist, for instance, all were equal: rich, poor, master, slave—even, as in Quodvultdeus here, dressed alike with similar demeanor. To obliterate all distinction was to announce a social revolution. For discussion, see Finn, *Liturgy of Baptism in*

Chrysostom, 83–85. Interestingly, Quodvultdeus invokes the equality of birth from the book of Wisdom—fittingly, since the competents are soon to be reborn.

9. The phrase is *sacramentum symboli* and here refers to one of the two rites having to do with the creed, possibly both (*traditio* and *redditio symboli*). The competents had received the creed a week earlier, also during a Saturday night vigil, in a rite called "the handing over of the creed" *(traditio symboli).* They were given the baptismal creed orally, article by article together with a brief explanation. During the following week, the competents, with the help of family and sponsors, sought to memorize what they had heard. Augustine, in a homily during the *traditio,* for instance, says that "the creed is the rule of faith briefly comprised to instruct the mind but not to burden the memory" (*Serm.* 213.1 [PL 38.1060]). As Augustine says in the next homily (*Serm.* 214.1 [PL 38.1066]), delivered on the same occasion, the purpose was to build up the competents' faith, to prepare for the profession of the creed, yet not to weigh the memory down. This profession, made publicly and known as the *redditio symboli,* is the rite that occasions this present homily of Quodvultdeus.

10. In the next century, the *vexilla crucis* would become a celebrated hymn, *Vexilla regis prodeunt,* which celebrated the mystery of Christ triumphant on the cross. The hymn was composed by the last of the representative Latin poets in Gaul, Venantius Fortunatus, bishop of Poitiers (d. 610), chaplain and friend of Queen Radegunda, who founded the monastery of the Holy Cross. The occasion of its composition was the arrival of the relic of the true cross sent to the queen by Emperor Justin II in 560. Quodvultdeus returns to the *vexilla* theme below in *De symb.* 3.5.2 (CCL 60.356) and note.

11. The second pivotal rite, renunciation of Satan, followed immediately upon the scrutiny as its logical conclusion, so to speak. The formula given here varied from church to church. In Ambrose's Milan it was interrogatory: "When you were asked: 'Do you renounce the devil and his works,'—what did you reply? 'I do renounce ...'" (*De sacramentis* 1.5 [PL 16.419] tr. Finn). An ancient rite, perhaps biblical, the significance in both East and West is invariable: renunciation of the religious aspects of pagan culture, especially the "games and spectacles" of the circus/amphitheater and theater, which remained a fatal attraction of popular culture. See the introduction ("The Pivotal Rites") and below, *De symb.* 1.1.19–2.15 (CCL 60.307–8) and notes, a theme to which Quodvultdeus returns repeatedly in these homilies.

12. The "book of life" imagery is, by Quodvultdeus's time, traditional and based on Rev 3:5; 13:8; 17:8; 20:12, 15; and 21:27; but as is clear from what follows, Quodvultdeus is evoking the rites of enlistment in the legions, which had two stages, *probatio* and *signatio.* The first, *probatio,* consisted of an examination of the recruit's *(tiro)* qualifications, including a stiff medical exam, certification of his status (free and citizen), and inquiry into his char-

acter. Were he to pass scrutiny, the provincial governor (an authority much higher than the recruiting officer) would approve and dispatch the recruit as a *probatus* to his assigned unit, where he began four months of intensive basic training. Next came the second stage, *signatio.* If he passed all his proficiency tests, the recruit became a qualified and fully trained legionary *(miles).* He received his *signaculum,* a lead tag bearing a seal and his name worn around his neck, took the formal military oath *(sacramentum),* and had his name and distinguishing physical traits, the names of his references, and the governor's name inscribed on the records of the unit as well as at headquarters (the higher heavenly power). The celebration that marked his becoming a *signatus* was a "passing out" parade, at which the commanding officer might give the kind of exhortation that now follows. The recruit could now be paid as a soldier. For amplification, see *Service in the Roman Army,* ed. Roy W. Davies, David Breeze, and Valerie A. Maxfield (New York: Columbia University Press, 1989), 3–23.

13. The reference, *voluptatem turpissimae delectationis,* appears to be the degrading "spectacles" Quodvultdeus is about to inveigh against: the shows in the theater (comedies/farces), the amphitheater (hunts and gladiatorial combat), the circus (chariot races), and stadium (athletic contests). Amphitheater is a synonym for circus, but may have been a separate building in Carthage, since Quodvultdeus speaks of circus and amphitheater. The former he identifies with the chariot races, and the latter, with the hunts and gladiatorial contests. See also below, *De symb.* 3.1.14–21 (CCL 60.350–51). Quodvultdeus and his predecessors (and even some classical Roman authors) were deeply offended by the religious character, wanton cruelty, violence, and immorality of the spectacles, as is evident in the passages and notes that follow. The earliest known amphitheater (c. 80 BCE) was built in Pompeii and called by its builders *spectacula*—hence the traditional name "spectacles." The remains of a striking example can be seen in El-Jem, south and east of Carthage, and the circus at Carthage is under excavation (see n. 17 below). In the West, Irenaeus was the first to attack the spectacles as idolatrous (*Adv. haer.* 1.1.2); Tertullian, however, devoted the better part of an entire work to the out-and-out indictment of the spectacles as idolatrous (*De spect.* 5–13 [CSEL 20.6–16]). In the final section Tertullian attacks them, as does Quodvultdeus, on moral grounds: They induce lust, frenzy, and cruelty (14–17 [CSEL 20.16–19]).

14. As we have seen in the introduction above (see under "Religious Turmoil: Pagans and Paganism"), Augustine addresses the addictive and blinding character of the games in the *Confessions,* when he comments on his pupil and friend Alypius, who was caught in the "whirlpool of Cathaginian morals, with their passion for empty public shows *[nugatoria spectacula]* that had sucked him into the folly of the circus games" (*Conf.* 6.7.11 [O'Donnell 1:64]). Augustine calls them "an incredible obsession," and Quodvultdeus, a

"rat-trap" *(muscipulam spectaculorum)*, an allusion to 1.10 (CCL 60.306) and Ps 123:7–8.

15. The term is *cavea*/cave, referring to the seats for the audience, rising row upon row to the top, but also alluding to the devil's lair/cave. In the *Lex Julia Theatralis*, Augustus prescribed the order of the seating: the fourteen rows of the orchestra were reserved for the highborn; the soldiers had their own section, as did married men and freeborn boys. Women might be present at the back of the theater. See Elizabeth Rawson, *"Discrimina Ordinum: The Lex Julia Theatralis,"* in *Roman Culture and Society: Collected Papers of Elizabeth Rawson* (Oxford: Clarendon Press, 1991), 508–45. Until the construction of the first permanent (stone), the "Theater of Pompey" (55 BCE)–disguised as a temple–Roman theaters were temporary wooden structures. With the accession of Augustus, however, theaters became monumental public buildings; by the end of the first century cities with as few as fifteen thousand inhabitants could boast a theater. Surviving North African examples are at Leptis Magna and Sabratha; but see Richard C. Beacham, *The Roman Theatre and Its Audience* (Cambridge, MA: Harvard University Press, 1992), 154–98.

16. Tertullian seems to have initiated this kind of counterargument. In *De spec.* 29–30 (CSEL 20.27–29), he proposes "literature of our own" (verses, maxims, songs, and melodies), the boxing and wrestling involved in the acquisition of virtue, the second coming, and the last judgment as the "spectacles of reality."

17. The term in the text is *circi/circus*; an equivalent term, as noted in n. 13 above, is *amphitheatrum* (in Greek, *hippodromos*). The circus was primarily for the chariot races; the amphitheater, for animal hunts and other extravaganzas, such as mock naval battles. Although there were five such buildings in Rome, the most famous is the *Amphitheatrum Florium* in Rome's Forum, since the early Middle Ages called the *Colosseum*. The most celebrated is the *Circus Maximus*, built between the Palatine and Aventine hills in Rome. The *Circus Vaticanus* (completed by Nero), perhaps the most venerable, is where St. Peter is reputed to have been killed and buried and where the basilica of St. Peter's now stands. The circus at Carthage is under excavation, but its outlines indicate a monumental building perhaps as vast as the *Circus Maximus*, which is reputed to have held one hundred thousand spectators. It may well be that Carthage's circus, given its vast size, could accommodate both the races and the hunts and so on. But see Naoimi Norman, "Excavations in the Circus at Carthage," *Archaeology* 40 (1987): 46–57. The circus at El-Jem, which is still in use for events such as rock concerts, had the hunt clearly in mind. Perhaps the circus at Carthage was also an amphitheater. In any case, at Rome the front seats at the circus, as at the theater, were reserved for senators, the next fourteen rows for the knights, with vestal vir-

gins and distinguished people of all kinds also in the front rows. Clearly the high-profile people in Carthage occupied the "good" seats.

18. For a detailed yet fascinating description of a chariot race, its symbolism, and its economics, see Roland Auguet, *Cruelty and Civilization: The Roman Games* (London: George Allen & Unwin, 1972), 120-48. What Quodvultdeus describes here tallies with Auguet's description. Normally, there were four teams in the race, designated by their team colors: the whites, the reds, the greens, and the blues. Auguet reports that a find at Douggha in North Africa reveals that a charioteer named Eros wore green, and a pavement mosaic in Carthage, possibly from the headquarters of the faction, bears the inscription *FELIX POPULUS VENETI,* translated in slang, "Up with the Blues" (ibid., 139). His thesis about the factions is that the "hippomania" (accurately recorded by Quodvultdeus) was induced by allegiance to the team more than by the races themselves.

19. Literally, processions or solemn parades, *pompa,* most often simply transliterated, "pomps." The games were religious in origin and spirit. The races, for instance—Quodvultdeus's concern here—were preceded by *pompa,* which mixed the processional order with ancient customs prescribing sacrifices. At Rome, the parade started at the capitol, crossed the Forum and reached the Circus Maximus, making the rounds of the stadium to the plaudits of the crowd. They would see the magistrate who gave the games leading the procession in a magnificent chariot. A purple toga adorned him and a slave stood behind him holding a golden crown over his head. The young men of noble Rome, both mounted and afoot, surrounded him. Next came the chariots and charioteers, and after them, the statues of the gods, some of which represented attributes of the gods and were driven in decorated chariots by children. Other statues—gods and demigods—might be perched in litters. Astride them were deified emperors (or generals) and particularly revered women, like Fausta, the wife of Antoninus Pius. Behind the statues came the priests and consuls, and swirling about were troupes of musicians and dancers, who moved rhythmically to the lyres. See Auguet, *Cruelty and Civilization,* 126–28. For the antiquity of the renunciation in early Christianity, see M. E. Boismard, "'I Renounce Satan, his Pomps, and his Works,'" in *Baptism in the New Testament: A Symposium,* tr. D. Askew (Baltimore: Helicon, 1964), 107–14.

20. Unlike Greek drama, which in large measure sought to instruct or inspire reflection, Roman drama sought primarily to entertain. By the middle of the second century BCE, theater and the games had joined forces, and theater became one of the spectacles. By the beginning of our era, tragedy and comedy had lost their popular appeal, and other genres took their place: farces with their stereotyped buffoonery, coarse and obscene jests, horseplay, and slapstick; mimes with their improvisations, low-brow humor, banter, and emphasis on sex and parody; and pantomimes, in which the performers

sought to tell a story, characterize a person or situation, or depict emotion through bodily movement. In late antiquity, according to Richard Beacham, the "virtuosity and titillation of the mime and the visual grace and splendor of the pantomime" usurped center stage, and the theater became "a medium of sensation rather than of thought" (*Roman Theatre,* 151). The mime and the pantomime—which had immense appeal in Carthage and elsewhere in the empire until the Vandal depredations—were Quodvultdeus's subject at this point in the homily. Carthage's theater was destroyed by the Vandals in 439. I am grateful to Rev. Michael W. Heintz for the following reference: Karen E. Ros, "The Roman Theater at Carthage" (Diss., University of Michigan, 1990).

21. The church saw the theater as enemy partly because the performers often satirized the church and its practices and parodied its rituals and beliefs. Indeed, in 452, mimes were excommunicated. But the subject matter of mimes and pantomimes also offended on moral grounds. Although Tertullian reserved his condemnations of theater for its idolatry (*De spec.* 10), he records with some horror the fact that the actor who once played the part of Hercules was actually castrated on stage (*Apol.* 15.5). Nude dancing was not unheard of even in Cicero's time (*In Catalinam* 2.23.26), and Apuleius recounts the seductive scene that opens the performance of the "Judgment of Paris" (*Metamorphoses* 8.30). It is reported that the emperor Elagabulus even ordered sexual scenes enacted rather than feigned (Aelian, *Varia historia* 25.4). All cited in Beacham, *Roman Theatre,* 137, 242 n. 77). Quodvltdeus, along with his colleagues in the world of baptismal catechesis, stands clearly in the line of moral condemnation.

22. Quodvultdeus here seems to echo what was said in the previous note about wanton sex on stage. Mimes could be men or women, and the latter performed scantily clad, sometimes nude.

23. Quodvultdeus may have in mind the story of Daedalus and his son, Icarus, sometimes enacted on stage. The father had constructed two pairs of wings from wax for them to escape from King Minos. Icarus flew too close to the sun; the wax melted, and he drowned. In any case, by Quodvultdeus's time the theater had become literally a place of spectacle. There were several devices the permitted actors to perform in the air: the *pregma,* about which Juvenal says that it could spirit boys away; the *geranos,* a device let down from above to lift up a performer; and the *aorai,* which were ropes that hung down to raise up heroes and gods to the heavens—their apotheosis (see Beacham, *Roman Theatre,* 180–82).

24. The story is about the birth of Isaac and Rebekah's sons, Esau and Jacob, an event that the author of Genesis understands as the portrayal of the history of two peoples, Edom and Israel. In the Hebrew text there is a play on the root (*'qb*) found in Jacob's name, "the heel-gripper." The issue is about Esau's birthright as firstborn, which Jacob secures by trickery. In Quodvultdeus's interpretation, as we are about to see (the *magni sacramenti*

figura) is not Edom/Israel; rather, the Jews are Edom, and Israel the church. This is an example of the "hermeneutical Jew" discussed in the introduction (see under "Religious Turmoil: The Jews and Judaism").

25. The direct reference is to baptism as birth from the baptismal womb of the church, and also to the liturgical embrace by the community, often called the "kiss of peace." The reference, however, evokes an actual Roman birth rite. The principal actors included the midwife and the father, who lifted up the infant to signify that he accepted the child as his own and that he would "raise" it.

26. For a general discussion of the amphitheaters in North Africa, as well as a more detailed analysis of the one in Carthage, see David Bomgardner, "An Analytic Study of North African Amphitheaters" (diss., University of Michigan, 1985)—a reference for which I am grateful to Rev. Michael W. Heintz of the University of Notre Dame.

27. The reference is to Cyprian's *Ad Donatum* 7–8 (CSEL 3.1.8–10). He refers to Carthaginian young men of substance, not to gladiators or condemned criminals. In the treatise, which principally concerns grace and his conversion (CE 246), Cyprian reflects on the brutal world from which he considered himself delivered, a world symbolized by the gladiatorial combats and the hunt *(venatio)*. For detailed discussion, see Auguet, *Cruelty and Civilization*, 81–106.

28. Quodvultdeus's reference is to Dan 14:30–42, which describes Daniel's battle with the dragon and reflects the Theodotion version of the Greek Bible, a text from which Quodvultdeus's biblical manuscripts seem to be translated. It is deuterocanonical in Catholic Bibles, but is listed among the Apocrypha in other versions as the final part of "Bel and the Dragon." The account of the lion's den is Dan 6:10–28.

29. The *venatio* was extremely popular in Carthage and evoked much passion in the amphitheater. Many hunters were killed in combat, as a number of unearthed lead curse plates and the remains in the circus at Carthage show, some of which are exhibited in the small archeological museum in Dermesh, a suburb of modern Tunis. The prosperous animal trade was in the hands of numerous well-organized associations. And *Nika* (Victory!) was the shout, as a number of wine jugs proclaim. The floor mosaics in the *villa* district, high above Carthage and the ancient port, depict the animals, the hunters, and the skills required in the hunt. In addition, they suggest the great popularity of the hunt. Quodvultdeus provides a rare firsthand picture of what went on.

30. Having commented on the rite of renunciation, Quodvultdeus now turns his attention to an extended commentary on the creed as it had been professed in the rite of *redditio symboli*. In Augustine's Hippo the creed was confided verse by verse to the competents in the *traditio symboli* during a homily very like the homily during a vigil held on the previous Saturday

night, as it must as have been in Carthage. The text is reconstructed in the introduction (see under "The Pivotal Rites"); Quodvultdeus generally gives the article to be commented on at the beginning of each section, which is signaled by brackets.

31. In the Neoplatonic world that prevailed in late antique intellectual culture with its doctrine of emanation, creation out of nothing would have been a meaningless, if not offensive, doctrine. For emanation, especially in Plotinus, see J. M. Rist, *The Road to Reality* (Cambridge: Cambridge University Press, 1967), 63–83; and Mark J. Edwards, "Neoplatonism," *ATAE* 588–91. Creation out of nothing remained a great philosophical puzzle among many Jews, Muslims, and Christians until well into the Middle Ages.

32. The phrase is *qui etiam ipsi creaturae convenientibus gradibus per diversas ordinationes constituit potestates.* Quodvultdeus has the ancient's view of creation, namely, that the world has no gaps in it. What appear to be empty spaces are filled with invisible powers *(potestates)* that have their sway over creation. They are appropriately graded *(convenientibus gradibus),* reflecting Plotinus's view that all modes of being—material, mental, temporal, and eternal—are established through the overflow of a single immaterial and impersonal force. As the One, it is the ground of all that exists; as the Good, it is the ground of all values. The closer one stands to the One or the Good, the more being or value one has. Such is the chain of being.

33. Quodvultdeus's initial concern is with the megalithic polytheism of the Greco-Roman religions of Carthage (reflected in the archaeological remains), which the catechist considers excluded by this first article of the creed. See the discussion in the introduction (under "Religious Turmoil: Pagans and Paganism"). Next he turns to the heretics, specifically, the Arians.

34. The Arians, Homoians, are discussed in the introduction (under "Religious Turmoil: Heretics"). In response to Quodvultdeus's request, Augustine composed *De haeresibus* (PL 42.21–50; CCL 46.286–345), listing and briefly discussing eighty-eight groups, including the original Arians and their heirs (Aetians, Semiarians, and Macedonians). He finds that they (1) deny that Father, Son, and Spirit are of the same essence, (2) assert that the Son and Spirit are creatures, (3) affirm that the Son took human flesh but not a soul, (4) hold that the Spirit is created from the Son, and (5) require that catholics be rebaptized. From what follows in Quodvultdeus, the Arians appear to have been a far more pressing problem in Carthage than in Hippo, for, as Michael Slusser observes, Augustine's *De trinitate* shows little relationship with or concern for the Arians ("Traditional Views of Late Arians," in *Arianism after Arius: Essays on the Development of the Fourth Century Trinitarian Conflicts,* ed. Michel R. Barnes and Daniel H. Williams [Edinburgh: T. & T. Clark, 1993], 5).

35. The Arian argument, largely based on scripture, appears to have been phrased in a slogan: *Pater maior est, filius minor est,* and, as

Quodvultdeus will indicate shortly (below, 1.9.6 [CCL 60.326]), *spiritus multo inferior*. Although the Arian controversy theoretically had been settled fifty years earlier at the Council of Constantinople (381), all the barbarian tribes who invaded the western empire in the fourth and fifth centuries were Arian Christians, primarily Homoian, including the Vandals. Arianism was in the North African air, and possibly some of Quodvultdeus's audience, including catechumens, were or had been Arian.

36. The reference is to the first rite of passage in Roman family life, which Susanne Dixon describes: "The new born child, once pronounced fit to live, probably by the midwife, would then be placed on the ground for the *paterfamilias* to raise up ritually as his indication that he accepted his paternity of the child and wished to rear it" (*The Roman Family* [Baltimore: Johns Hopkins University Press, 1992], 108). Thus the phrase: *et quilibet pater antequam suscipiat filium, non vocabitur pater*.

37. The term in the text is *dignitatem*. For Quodvultdeus and his audience, it evokes paternal power *(patriapotestas)*, which was the organizing principle of the Roman law of persons and property. Among the powers, it included the father's right of life and death over his descendants, his right of ownership of the family's property, and his right to disinherit. These paternal rights or powers ceased only with the death of the father; only then could the son achieve them. In that "eternal generation" this is not the case. For paternal power, see Richard P. Saller, *Patriarchy, Property and Death in the Roman Family* (Cambridge: Cambridge University Press, 1994), 114–30.

38. One of the characteristics of the Homoians was that they emphasized the data in scripture and avoided the metaphysical and logical analysis of their eastern Arian brethren. Thus, in all three homilies Quodvultdeus emphasizes scripture and its analysis.

39. Quodvultdeus had elided some of Matthew, namely, that the Son of Man will come with all his angels and that he will be seated on the seat of his majesty.

40. The reference is to Christ's human nature, a way of speaking grounded in the Dyophysite, or so-called Nestorian, dispute of the period and rooted in the classical Christology of Theodore of Mopsuestia (d. 428) and the Antiochene school. Theodore and his followers often spoke of Christ as the "Man-Assumed" to designate (and emphasize) his human nature; see Aloys Grillmeyer, *Christ in Christian Tradition*, vol. 1, *From the Apostolic Age to Chalcedon (451)*, tr. John Bowden (Atlanta: John Knox Press, 1975), esp. 421–39. Normal Latin usage would be *homo assumptus*, but here it is *homo susceptus*, the very terminology Quodvultdeus used when speaking of the rite of initiation in which the father raised up his infant to assent to his paternity and to signify his commitment to raising the child. See n. 36 above, and below, 1.6.21; CCL 60.322 (where Quodvultdeus, speaking of Jesus' resurrection, says *filium Dei facit te*) and note.

41. The Vulgate text is identical, but Quodvultdeus (and perhaps, his African tradition) understands *sanctus spiritus* as the Holy Spirit, which makes the translation awkward at best, for the natural sense is "the holy and learned spirit will flee falsehood."

42. The translation can only distantly reflect the author's alliterations: *quia genetrix suum genuit genitirem, quia creavit creatura factorem?* (CCL 60.317). The question registers what continued to be a raging controversy in the East, namely, whether Mary can properly be called the "Mother of God" *(Theotokos)*, a controversy usually called "Nestorian" but more properly called "Dyophysite," which has separated the Church of the East from the Orthodox and the Catholics until recently. As of 1994, the Church of the East (also called the Assyrian Church of the East) has affirmed with the Roman Catholic Church that Christ possesses both "divine and human natures that retain their own properties, faculties, and operations unconfusedly, immutably, undividedly, and inseparably" (see www.cired.org [1999]).

43. For this kind of kenotic theology, see also Ambrose, *Expl. symb.* 3 (CSEL 73.5); and Augustine, *De fide et symbolo* 8 (CSEL 41.11).

44. See below, *De symb.* 2.4.2–6 (CCL 60.338–39). The doctrine of Mary's virginal conception is found widely during the second century in the creeds, the Apocrypha, and apologists such as Justin Martyr, Irenaeus, and Clement of Alexandria, who draw the parallel between Eve and Mary. A cognate doctrine of the same century, that the signs of Mary's virginity were preserved even through childbirth *(virginitas in partu)*, appears in the Apocrypha *(Odes of Solomon* 19, *Protoevangelium of James* 19, 20), which yielded the doctrine of Mary's perpetual virginity. Augustine, in *Serm.* 215.3, asks: "For who is able properly to understand that God chose to be born among men, that a virgin conceived without male seed, gave birth without breaking [the hymen], and retained it unbroken after birth?" (PL 38.1075, tr. Finn). See Michael O'Carroll, "Virginity of Mary, Virginity in Partu," *Theotokos,* 357–62.

45. Implied is the typology of Mary as Jerusalem/Sion, which is also in Augustine, whom Quodvultdeus seems to be following in the subsequent commentary. Commenting on this verse (5) Augustine calls attention to the great mystery: the man who is born in Sion is Christ, "man for our sakes, God before us"; and Sion is his mother: "As he founded a city in which he was born, so he created a mother from whom he was born" *(Enarrationes in Psalmos* 86.7–8 [PL 37.1106–7; CCL 39.1057–58] tr. Finn).

46. Reading this passage from Quodvultdeus with the Roman Catholic doctrine of Mary's immaculate conception, some might understand it as a witness to her freedom from original sin, an exemption that seems based on the patristic doctrine of Mary as the New Eve. Explicit testimony about freedom from sin arises first with Ephraem Syrus (307–373) in his *Nisibene Hymns* (CSCO 218.61; 219.76). Augustine, with his view of orginal sin transmitted by intercourse, thought that no sin could be mentioned where Mary

was concerned (*De natura et gratia* 36.42 [PL 44.267), but his meaning seems best understood as that Christ was free from original sin. In any case, in this period, Ephraem, Augustine, and Quodvultdeus are witnesses to the holiness and sinlessness of Mary. See Michael O'Carroll, "Immaculate Conception," *Theotokos,* 179–82.

47. See the introduction (under "Religious Turmoil"). *Adversus Judaeos* literature abounded in the patristic period, as noted above, emerging first in Tertullian's work (CSEL 70.251–331). He wrote more to refute than to condemn the Jews of Carthage. Quodvultdeus clearly condemns in the diatribe that follows, calling the Jews "Christ-killers." See also below, *De symb.* 2.5.11–14 (CCL 60.342), and Quodvultdeus's *Adversus quinque haereses* 4.1–41 (CCL 40.268–76), and his *Contra Judaeos* 18:1–14 (CCL 40.252–54). For Augustine's anti-Judaism and a brief account of the patristic background, see Jeremy Cohen, *Living Letters of the Law: Ideas of the Jew in Medieval Christianity* (Berkeley: University of California Press, 1999), 1–65.

48. Quodvultdeus returns to the murder of the Innocents below in *De symb.* 2.4.10 (CCL 60:339) and 3.4.14–19 (CCL 60.355).

49. The translation does not reflect the irony in the text, which reads, *sic furias vestras vestrique regis susannabat....*The *furias* are the "Furies" (Erinyes), those chthonian powers of retribution for wrongs and blood-guilt especially in the family, individually or collectively carrying out the curses of a mother or father. Thus, Quodvultdeus literally says, "thus does he mock your furies and those of the king."

50. These two passages (24 and 25) bear a striking resemblance to Augustine, *De fid. et symb.* 4.9 (CSEL 41.12–13).

51. The image Quodvultdeus now develops is complex and striking: the crucifixion as the marriage of Christ and the church. Especially striking is the image below of the cross as the nuptial bed (6.3–6 [CCL 60.320]). The root idea is the covenant, which the prophets like Hosea often portrayed as a marriage contract. The crucifixion (blood of the New Covenant) here in Quodvultdeus simply continues the idea. Just as the first covenant was sealed by the blood of circumcision, so the second is sealed by the blood of crucifixion. But the context of the image is baptism. The blood of Christ crucified makes baptism effective. The imagery is shaped by a long-hallowed typology that sees, as if through a transparency, the crucified Christ, the rites of baptism, the newly baptized, and the church all together. As Jean Daniélou puts it: "Baptism is seen in its fullness as a nuptial mystery" (*The Bible and the Liturgy* [Notre Dame: University of Notre Dame Press, 1956], 200; see 191–207). In the baptismal pool, the candidates become the brides, whom Christ purifies through his blood shed on the cross. They have plighted to him their love and allegiance in professing the creed; they have renounced their former suitor, Satan; their old self is stripped off; and they are adorned in a new, white-robed self, as if in a marriage garment. By the fourth century

the typology was well developed in both the Greek-speaking East (Cyril of Jerusalem, John Chrysostom, and Gregory of Nyssa) and the Latin-speaking West (Ambrose and Augustine). For the development, see Jean Daniélou, *From Shadows to Reality: Studies in the Biblical Typology of the Fathers,* tr. Wulstan Hibberd (London: Burns and Oates, 1960), 131–49; and for Chrysostom and his contemporaries, see T. M. Finn, *The Liturgy of Baptism in the Baptismal Instructions of St. John Chrysostom,* SCA 15 (Washington, DC: Catholic University of America Press, 1967), 158–66; and idem, *Early Christian Baptism,* 10–11.

52. The Fathers of the Church said little about marriage, and when they did it was about marriage as an important aspect of Christian life, not as an ecclesiastical institution. For the development of the marriage rites, see John K. Leonard, "Rites of Marriage in the Western Middle Ages," in *Medieval Liturgy: A Book of Essays,* ed. Lizette Larson-Miller, Garland Medieval Casebooks (New York/London: Garland, 1997), 165–202. When Christians, as Roman citizens, married it was under the civil laws and customs observed at the time; the legal regulations about marriage and divorce were left to the government. An important function of marriage was the transfer of property and social standing. As a result, finding the "right" bride or the "right" groom was no light undertaking, as Quodvultdeus recognizes in this passage. The father would naturally consult friends, kinsmen, and his wife before arranging a marriage for his son or daughter; the mother too would circulate her network of friends and relatives to check up on reputation, family, and prospects. The matchmakers could rely, however, on long-established criteria. For a man the list included birth, hometown, connections, wealth, morals, and affection for the potential bride; for a woman, birth, wealth, beauty, charm, fertility, and chastity. Disparity of birth between bride and groom was to be avoided at all costs. For detailed discussion, see Susan Treggiari, "Ideals and Practicalities in Matchmaking in Ancient Rome," in *The Family in Antiquity to the Present,* ed. David I. Kertzer and Richard P. Saller (New Haven: Yale University Press, 1991), 91–108.

53. See below, *De symb.* 2.4.27 (CCL 60.340–41) and 3.4.7; (CCL 60.354).

54. The figure of the Lamb revealed in Rev 5:6 continually thereafter stands behind this section. Indeed, in Rev 19:9, the eschatological banquet is identified as the marriage supper for the Lamb. A few lines later, the white-robed army of the martyrs appears (Rev 8:9; 22:14), which evokes the linen garments the newly baptized will soon put on. Revelation was an extremely important work in Carthaginian Christianity, the subject of commentary by Tyconius (d. c. 400), the celebrated, older North African contemporary of Augustine, who was a Donatist lay theologian and perceptive interpreter of the Bible. His *Liber Regularum* deeply influenced Augustine (see *De doctrina christiana* 30.42) and through him early medieval interpreters like Bede. See

Pamela Bright, *The Book of Rules of Tyconius: Its Purpose and Inner Logic,* Christianity and Judaism in Antiquity 2 (Notre Dame, IN: University of Notre Dame Press, 1988), 1–33; and Charles Kannengiesser, "Augustine and Tyconius: A Conflict of Christian Hermeneutics in Roman Africa," in *Augustine and the Bible,* ed. Pamela Bright, Bible through the Ages 2 (Notre Dame, IN: University of Notre Dame Press, 1999), 149–77.

55. The text reads *gemina sacramenta* (CCL 60.320). Quodvultdeus invokes a tradition hallowed in both East and West that the church is formed from the water (baptism) and the blood (Eucharist) that flow from Christ's pierced side. Such is the source of their efficacy (see Chrystostom, *Cat. bapt.* 3.16–22 [Wenger, SC 50.160–64] and Augustine, *De civ. Dei* 22.17 [CCL 48.835–36]). For a study of the tradition, see Alban Maguire, *Blood and Water: The Wounded Side of Christ in Early Christian Literature,* SST 108 (Washington, DC: Catholic University of America Press, 1958). But note the complex richness with which Quodvultdeus develops the tradition in what follows: The cross is the nuptial bed, and the wound in side of Christ, the virginal Bridegroom, is, like Mary's vagina, the opening through which the church, as virginal bride, is born. The account in Genesis must be kept in mind here as it was clearly in Quodvultdeus's mind: Adam brings forth Eve, whom he marries as one somehow already a part of him.

56. Quodvultdeus here reflects Augustine's doctrine of redemption and grace as gratuitous. See below, *De symb.* 3.5.9–11 (CCL 60.356), where Quodvultdeus understands "so great a mystery" to be that the Mediator, mingling in himself God and man, joined God and humans. For Augustine on grace and redemption, see J. Patout Burns, "Grace," *ATAE* 391–98.

57. The direct reference is the rite of initiation for the newborn; in this case, for the Christian, the rites of baptism. But for the audience it would evoke also the rites of initiation of the newborn into the family, when the father of a child lifted the infant up to signify that he both accepted the infant as his and was committed to raising it. See above, *De symb.* 1.3.21 (60.312), and note. But the allusion is also to what in the East is called *theosis* and in the West, *deificatio,* and about which Augustine, reflecting a long-standing Greek and Latin tradition, wrote that the one who was God was made man to make humans God (*Serm.* 192.1.1). But see G. Bonner, "Deification, Divinization," *ATAE* 265–66.

58. The vulgate text is similar to Quodvultdeus's text *(et synagoga populorum circumdabit te et propter hanc in altum regredere dominus judicat populos),* but the point is not clear from the psalm's context, which depicts the petitioner pursued by enemies. The psalmist asks God to rise up against his enemies, and he petitions that the assembly of the peoples be gathered around him (God) as he comes to assume his judgment seat, and that he judge the petitioner and vindicate (the pslamist's) righteousness. Augustine comments

on the same text, also understanding it as a judgment scene (*Enar. Ps.* 7.7–8 [PL 36.101–3; CCL 38.40–42]).

59. The text reads, *quando absens ab eis in homine illo suscepto sentiris.* *Sentiris* appears to be a notary mistake. I have followed a variant reading, *sentiaris,* noting that Quodvultdeus contrasts "thought to be absent" with *praesentia tuae majestatis* in the next sentence. The Man-Assumed is actually present, even though he is thought to be absent. Three variant readings indicate that it is *per praesentia.* I follow the variant reading, because I take Quodvultdeus to mean that even though "absence makes the heart grow fonder" (more faithful), the Man assumed and now ascended remains present in the faithful.

60. Although the allusion is to Matt 8:17, that verse alludes to the Suffering Servant of Isa 53:4–5 (Vulgate): *vere languores nostros ipse tulit et dolores nostros ipse portavit et nos putavimus eum quasi leprosum et percussum a Deo et humiliatum ipse autem vulneratus est propter inquitates nostras adritus est propter scelera nostra disciplina pacis nostrae super eum et livore eius sanati sumus.* Indeed, this entire section (7.8–10), and the opposites with which Quodvultdeus has composed it, evokes the Suffering Servant motif of Isaiah and the Righteous Sufferer of the Psalms (as in Psalm 68, which Quodvultdeus has already cited above, 1.6.15 [CCL 60.321]).

61. Coming to judge in the form in which Christ was judged is important to Quodvultdeus. See below, *De symb.* 3.8.3–4 (CCL 60.360), where Zech 12:10 is quoted and John 19:37 cited: "They will look on the one whom they have pierced. The Jews then will see the God-man always reigning, the one whom they despised by denying him as he lay dying." See also Augustine, *Serm.* 214.9 (PL 38.1070–71), and the next note.

62. The Vulgate reads, *et aspicient ad me quem confixerunt,* whereas Quodvultdeus's text reads, *videbunt in quem pupugerunt.* By the end of the first century these words, which look ahead to a smitten Messiah, were already applied typologically to the crucified Christ (thus John 19:37). Augustine applies the verse as does Quodvultdeus, but briefly, and cites the verse as follows: *[Et itermum alia Scriptura dicit,] Videbunt in quem confixerunt* (*In Joh.* 120.3 [PL 35.1953; CCL 36.661–62]). Quodvultdeus's implied emphasis is on seeing; in Augustine, the emphasis is explicit, because the point is about the sight that faith yields (*In Joh.* 21.5 [PL 35.1958–59]).

63. Quodvultdeus recalls here the *gemina sacramenta,* baptism and the Eucharist, for which see above, 1.6.5 (CCL 60.320), and n. 55.

64. The verbs are singular, but I have translated the subject, *unusquisque,* as a corporate plural.

65. Quodvultdeus speaks of the double procession of the Spirit from the Father and the Son almost as a matter of course. See also below, *De symb.* 3.9.1 (CCL 60.360) and note. Indeed, for Augustine it was a settled matter. Quodvultdeus's passage here has an Augustinian ring to it: He cites the same

108 QUODVULTDEUS OF CARTHAGE

New Testament verses, speaks of Spirit of the Father and of the Son, and implies that the Spirit is the gift of both Father and Son. That the Spirit proceeded from the Father and the Son (filioque) was a central part of Augustine's theology and led to his reinterpretation of the baptismal creed in De fid. et symb. 9.16-18 (PL 40:189-90). But see Augustine, De trin. 5.11 (PL 42.918-19; CCL 50.218-20) and Allan D. Fitzgerald, "Filioque," ATAE 369-70. I am grateful to Rev. Michael W. Heintz for the following references in Augustine's sermons and to G. Bonner: Serm. 2.12.2 (PL 38.1061; CCL 41): Per ipsum [Christum] nobis Spiritus Sanctus missus est a Patre, et ab ipso. Spiritus et Filii ab utroque missus ... ille Spiritus Patris et Filii; Serm. 214.10: Credimus enim in Spiritum sanctum de Patre procedentem, nec tamen Filium; super Filium manentem, nec Filii patrem; de Filii [sic] accipientem, nec tamen Filii filium. For Augustine's pneumatology, in addition to Fitzgerald's "Filioque," see. G. Bonner, "St. Augustine's Doctrine of the Holy Spirit," Sobornost 4 (1960): 51-66.

66. See above, De symb. 1.3.9-4.38 (CCL 60.310-17), which deals with the Father and Son, and 1.13.3-13 (CCL 60.333-34), which deals with Arian practices. In the passages that follow, Quodvultdeus completes his refutation of the Homoian Arian argument that Father, Son, and Spirit are hypostatically differentiated and subordinated, reflecting different statuses of being. Thus the Father is greater (maior), because only he exists from himself. The Son is less (minor), because he exists from the Father. The Spirit is much less (multo inferior), because he is subordinate to the Son. But these Arians, rather than appealing to metaphysical analysis, preferred to show how the scriptures depict Father, Son, and Spirit as distinct and individual entities. In the passages that follow, Quodvultdeus is concerned to refute the argument that the Spirit is clearly much inferior to the Son, because, while the Son appears as a man, the Spirit appears as a dove.

67. The reference is to metempsychosis, more accurately, metemsomatosis, very likely as taught by Neoplatonists. Plotinus, for instance, held that souls could reincarnate even in plants (Enn. 3.4.2). Augustine says that Plato held that after death the souls of men return to earth in a cycle and even into the body of animals, and that Porphyry, who rejected the idea of souls entering animals, held that they return to earth to enter human bodies—not their own but new and different bodies (De civ. Dei 10.39 [Loeb 3.394-95]). In Contra Celsum Origen notes that Pythagoras, Plato, and Empedocles held that each soul enters the kind of body its former life and character merited for it (1.32-33 [Henry Chadwick, Contra Celsum (Cambridge: Cambridge University Press, 1965), 32-33]).

68. Psalm 11:9 in the Vulgate reads: in circuitu impii ambulabunt cum exaltati fuerint vilissimi filiorum hominum. Although Quodvultdeus's reference is obscure, his meaning seems to be that the Arians think of the divine sub-

stance as they do of humans, cutting it down, so to speak, to human size. Nonetheless, he does not want to delay on the point.

69. Quodvultdeus uses *substantia* here and below in 9.27 (CCL 60.329), because, as he sees it, the Homoian argument must necessarily conclude to three gods. In 9.27 below he defines the catholic position in distinctly Augustinian terms: *Divina illa substantia trinitatis manens in se secuti est.*

70. In speaking of fire flaming up (which does not appear in the biblical text), Quodvultdeus means the *shekinah*, sometimes called the "pillar of cloud" in Exodus and sometimes, the "pillar of fire"—in either case, the reference is to the intimate and active divine presence.

71. Quodvultdeus still has the Arians in mind.

72. That correct faith about the Trinity is necessary for a valid baptism was a widespread conviction in and after the fourth century. Catholics challenged Donatists and Arians on this score, who in turn challenged catholics. Optatus of Milevis, the Numidian Catholic bishop whose work (c. 380) challenging the Donatists in the late fourth century had such a profound effect on the ecclesiology of the Western Church, argued that valid baptism has three components that constitute the sacrament: the action of the Trinity, the faith of the recipient, and the action of the minister. Only the first two were indispensable for its validity. In any effective baptism, for instance, the Trinity is the primary agent who accomplishes the blessings of the sacrament. Any defect of faith in the Trinity, then, invalidates the sacrament (see *De schis. Donat.* 5.4 [PL 11.1051–52]). But Optatus is concerned primarily about validity. Quodvultdeus's concern, however, was fruitfulness: Arian baptism, while valid, did not accomplish the grace of rebirth; because valid, rebaptism of Arians was not required for them to become Catholics. He holds, however, that catholic trinitarian faith is necessary for fruitful baptism. Augustine, arguing against the Donatists, had urged that baptism can be valid outside the church, but fruitful only within, because the church is the root of holiness (*De baptismo contra Donatistas* 1.10.13–12.19 [PL 43.116–19]). See J. Patout Burns, "On Rebaptism: Social Organization in the Third Century Church," *JEC* 1 (1993): 367–403; and William Harmless, "Baptism," *ATAE* 88.

73. Quodvultdeus, like Augustine (*De fid. et symb.* 10.21 [PL 40.193/ CSEL 41.28]: *quam vitam donec perfectam capiamus, sine peccatis esse non possumus*), thinks it impossible to live without sinning in this life.

74. This is a verse from Psalm 26, which was the psalm chanted during the scrutiny, an appropriate reminder by Quodvultdeus.

75. Quodvultdeus's image evokes the vision of Ezekiel (Ezek 3:12) and Elijah's chariot of fire (2 Kgs 2:11) as a transparency through which his audience could have a realistic sense of Christ's ascension and their own. See below, *De symb.* 3.11.5 (CCL 60.347). Quodvultdeus appears to be the only Latin patristic writer to use this imagery of death.

76. *Corruptio,* Quodvultdeus's word here, means literally "breaking into pieces"; only gradually did it come to mean a wasting or ruining or wearing down physically and morally. Quodvultdeus has in mind primarily the literal meaning—this is what constitutes the "weakness" *(infirmitas)* about which he is speaking. In any case, his point is that this tendency to fall apart, now part of the human condition, is not part of resurrection life.

77. The editor cites Ps 35:9, but in the Vulgate v. 10 reads: *quoniam tecum est fons vitae.* Very likely, Quodvultdeus is also reflecting John 7:37–38: "If any one thirsts, let him come to me. ... he who believes in me just as scripture says will have rivers of living water flowing from his stomach."

78. See below, *De symb.* 2.12.3–4 (CCL 60.348), where Quodvultdeus also contrasts what is not part of eternal life with what is at the heart of it. In ibid. 3.1-4 (CCL 60.352–53), he gives a brief summary of what is said in creedal homilies 1 and 2.

79. The reference is to 2 Cor 3:18, which speaks of being transformed from glory to glory.

80. In my view *manens secum* in context has the image of Christ, the celibate solitary. The entire sentence, however, is cryptic for two reasons: first, it is a veiled reference to Rev 14:4: "These are they [i.e., the 144,000] who have not defiled themselves with women; for they remain virgins. These are the ones who follow the Lamb." In his *Lib. prom., Gloria sanctorum* VI (CCL 60.217), Quodvultdeus cites this verse and comments: "Why the virgins follow, and why those who are not virgins cannot follow, the unbelievers will not understand." Second, its context is Donatist ecclesiology: the virgins are the martyrs, who comprise the true church; the nonvirgins are those who consorted with the imperial government—the *traditores.* The Donatist theologian Tyconius (c. 330–c. 390) developed an inclusive ecclesiology, for which the Donatists excommunicated him: the church, as universal, was bipartite, composed of saints and sinners until their definitive separation at the last judgment. See the discussion in W. H. C. Frend, *The Donatist Church: A Movement of Protest in Roman North Africa,* 3rd ed. (Oxford: Clarendon Press, 1987), 201-5. At all events, for Quodvultdeus, Christ does not desert those who are not martyrs, because the church is made up of both *virgines* and *nonvirgines,* which, especially in Donatist Africa, he concedes is difficult to understand and explain.

81. See above, *De symb.* 1.5.1–19 (CCL 60.317–19) and note; 2.4.27–28 (CCL 60.340–41) and notes; and 3.13.2–7 (CCL 60.363) and note. Recall the following three studies of the church as bride and mother: Plumpe, *Mater Ecclesia;* Bedard, *Symbolism of the Baptismal Font;* and Hugo Rahner, *Our Lady and the Church,* tr. Sebastian Bullock (New York: Pantheon, 1961), 45–68.

82. The reference to nourishment and nurture refers to the Eucharist and to the kind of homily Quodvultdeus is now about to conclude, "breaking the bread of the word." Signifying or marking the "children" as worthy of

God the Father evokes the sign of the cross often traced over the competents at the beginning their inscription, but especially the anointing in the form of a cross at the conclusion of baptism, for which see Harmless, *Augustine and the Catechumenate*, 310–11, and passim.

83. The sentence reads, *Tanta est, talis est, nobilis est, regia prole fecunda est*, with *talis* rhetorically placed, prompting the translation of *talis* and *noblis* in apposition.

84. Although Quodvultdeus has the Arians directly in mind, he is well aware of other heretics and schismatics, especially the Donatists and the long Donatist–catholic controversy, which came to a head at Carthage in CE 411 at a conference held under the presidency of the imperial legate (for the proceedings, see *Gesta collationis Cartagenensis* [PL 11.1225–1419; CCL 149A]; and Frend, *Donatist Church*, 275–89). Although the Donatist church lost its supremacy in North Africa as a result of the council, the Donatists retained their organization and strength largely in the villages, especially of Numidia, and among the Berber tribes. That there were former Donatists in Quodvultdeus's congregation, and some seeking admission and reconciliation, seems highly likely.

85. Clearly, the Arian is front and center in Quodvultdeus's mind. See below, *De symb.* 3.13.5 (CCL 60.363), where he mentions the harm the Arians do the church; and ibid. 3.9.10 (CCL 60.361), where he calls them wolves.

86. The allusion is to Gen 3:15, where God promises that the woman will strike the serpent's head. The wolf seems to be the Donatist and the viper, the Arian. In any case, he collapses them into one in what follows, with the Arian clearly in view.

87. Quodvultdeus records here the practices of Arian recruiters, about which little is known or documented.

88. For Quodvultdeus, the true mother is the Catholic church. Although Donatists and Arians each claimed to be the mother or true church, for Quodvultdeus they are churches that sit in a corner of the world as opposed to the catholic church, which is everywhere, situated in the whole world. As we have seen, in *Contra Judaeos*, he says, *Apud catholicam, dilectissime, noveritis esse tantum veram fidem, germanam pacem, perpetua salutem. Non enim in angulo est, sed ubique tota est* (20.1; CCL 60.255). In *De symb.* 3, he says about the Arians, *Quomodo exsultas, arriane, quod teneas veritatem, cum te malus error a catholica totius orbis secernenes, in uno angulo damnaverit?* adding in the chapter (13) on the church, *Ecclesia totum possidet, quod a viro suo acceptit in dote. Quecumque contregatio cuiuslibet haeresis in angulis sedet: concubina est, non matrona* (3.9.9 [CCL 60.361]; 3.13.4 [CCL 60.363]).

89. The term *exsufflas* here evokes the prebaptismal rite (exsufflation)—part of the renunciation of Satan—in which the renunciand turned to the west and "exsufflated" on Satan, the demon of the West. The action involved a hissing—breath mixed with saliva—thus, spitting (on Satan).

Given what immediately follows, Quodvultdeus could easily have in mind both the Donatists and the Arians; both required baptism anew of the catholic who sought to become a Donatist or an Arian (see nn. 90 and 91 below). I prefer the variant reading of ms B: "rebaptizing the Catholic, you spit on Christ."

90. Arians, according to Quodvultdeus, bribed Catholics to become Arian and, in so doing, killed them spiritually. The evidence for forced conversions is considerable on all sides—Catholic, Donatist, Arian, Goths, and finally Vandals—but the force in the Donatist controversy seems to be at the fore here. In 347, the imperial notaries Paul and Macarius sought forcibly to repress the Donatist church in Africa; the violence of the Donatist Circumcellions, who moved about in gangs armed with clubs and the watchword "Praise God" targeted catholic clergy and converts from Donatism. See W. H. C. Frend, "Circumcellions," *EEC* 1:175–76. On the subject of money, apart from benefits offered to prospective converts to Donatism and Arianism, there is no clear evidence of money changing hands. It is true that Donatists, especially Circumcellions, sold relics of both real and spurious martyrs (ibid.). There is no history of Arianism in the West comparable to that of Arianism in the East, for which see Thomas A. Kopecek, *A History of Neo-Arianism*, 2 vols., Patristic Monograph Series 8 (Cambridge, MA: Philadelphia Patristic Foundation, 1979); R. P. C. Hanson, *The Search for the Christian Doctrine of God: The Arian Controversy 318–381* (Edinburgh: T. & T. Clark, 1988). For discussions of rebaptism, see the next note.

91. Rebaptism was a central issue between Donatists and catholics. The Donatists held that the catholics, as the church of the *traditores*, were outside the true church. As such, they did not possess the Spirit of Holiness and could not, therefore, convey the Spirit. Catholic baptism was, therefore, of no avail, neither valid nor fruitful. For Catholics to become Donatists they had to be rebaptized. The Donatist position on rebaptism was deeply rooted in North African baptismal tradition, which held the invalidity of baptism given by heretics. Already, according to Augustine, it was an issue at the time of Cyprian's predecessor, Aggripinus, who held a council of the North African church (c. 220) that confirmed the practice of rebaptism of heretics. For the Donatists, however, Cyprian's teaching was determinative, as we learn from Augustine (*De bapt.* 2.9.14 [PL 43.135–37]). See J. Patout Burns, "On Rebaptism," *JEC* 1 (1993): 367–403, esp. 369–79; William Harmless, "Baptism," *ATAE* 88–89; and Maureen Tilley, *"De baptismo,"* *ATAE* 91–92.

92. Quodvultdeus seems to have in mind the discipline of public penance (Tertullian called it *exomologesis* [*De paen.* 9.1–2]), which one could enter voluntarily or by order of the bishop. It meant standing in the place of penitence in the church and being separated from the Eucharist. Clearly, the discipline could occasion bitterness. For penance and reconciliation in Augustine's Africa, see Allan D. Fitzgerald, "Penance," *ATAE* 640–46. For

studies of the history of the rite, see Bernhard Poschmann, *Penance and the Anointing of the Sick*, tr. Francis Courtney (New York: Herder and Herder, 1964), 44–121; and, more recently, Michael S. Driscoll, "Penance in Transition: Popular Piety and Practice," in *Medieval Liturgy*, ed. Larson-Miller, 120–63.

THE SECOND HOMILY ON THE CREED

1. The intriguing phrase here is *memoriaequae mandatum pro vestra salutem retinetuis*, which asserts an important link between memory and salvation, in this case, memory of the creed. But simple memorization is not Quodvultdeus's point. *Memoriaequae mandatum* refers to a kind of memorization which, according to classical rhetoricians, required that a work is to be memorized by being broken into pieces signaled by symbols or "memory markers." By using this technical phrase, Quodvultdeus is alerting his catechumens that he will preach in such a way as to accommodate their process of memorization. Thus, the phrases of the creed which appear in the sections that follow—belief in God the Father (2.1), etc.

2. The text agrees with the Vulgate word for word, but Quodvultdeus's biblical text is not Jerome's. As noted above in the introduction (under "The Scriptures"), it is one of the versions of the basic text of Tertullian, Cyprian, and Augustine, who calls it *Itala* (*Doctr. chr.* 2.15.22 [PL 34.46; CCL 32.47–48]: he says it is to be preferred to the others). It is also known as the African *Vetus Latina* or *Afra*.

3. The reference is to the rites of renunciation and profession, which the competents had enacted in scrutiny, during the vigil of the previous evening, for which see Quodvultdeus's extensive discussion above in *De symb.* 1.1.5–14 (CCL 60.305–6) and notes; see also the introduction (under "The Pivotal Rites"). Quodvultdeus's concern in what follows is idolatry, specifically, the *pompa*, for which see Tertullian, *De idol.* 6, 11, 18 (pomps), 13 (spectacles), 16 (solemnities) in PL 1.714–75 and CCL 1.227–53; *De spect.* 1–13 (PL 1.703–31 and CCL 2.1101–24), where he gives the origin and function of the games and festivals that take place in the theater and circus. For the renunciation in the East, see T. M. Finn, *The Liturgy of Baptism in the Baptismal Instructions of St. John Chrysostom*, SCA 15 (Washington, DC: Catholic University of America Press, 1967), 86–118. Quodvultdeus inveighs against the shows, circus, and theater, as we have seen in *De symb.* 1.1.17–2.20 (CCL 60.306–9) and notes.

4. Quodvultdeus comments obliquely on 1 John 2:16, adopting its triple form. The Vulgate speaks of *concupiscentia carnis, concupiscentia oculorum, superbiavitae...;* Quodvultdeus's African text speaks of *desideria carnis,*

desideria oculorum, ambitiones saeculi, which Quodvultdeus translates into his view of the Carthaginian world of public spectacles: *illecebrae voluptatis, nugacitas speculorum, insania superbia.* Augustine, as we have seen above, has equally scathing comments to make about Carthage's "empty public shows" and his friend Alypius's passion for them such that he was captivated by the blood-lust they induced in him (*Conf.* 6.11–13 [O'Donnell 1:68–70]).

5. Quodvultdeus seems to have in mind the formal details of the judicial system that involved the lighting of a brazier when the judge rendered sentence: he is suggesting that the magistrate is overcome with the smoke of power and pride more than of the fumes. But on the addictive power of the spectacles and Alypius, Augustine's friend, see *Conf.* 6.7.11–12 [O'Donnell 1:64]).

6. The reference is to the Carthaginian baptismal creed, which the competents had professed during the vigil the night before *(redditio symboli).* For the creed, see above, *De symb.* 1.3.1 (CCL 60.310), and the introduction (under *"Traditio symboli"*) and n. 22; see also below, *De symb.* 2.3.1 (CCL 60.310) and notes.

7. This famous Augustinian precept, here repeated by Quodvultdeus, was derived from the African version of Isaiah. It diverges considerably from the Vulgate, which reads *nisi credideritis, non permanebitis.* Augustine comments on his African version in *Serm.* 43 (PL 38:254–58): *De eo quod scriptum est in Isaia, cap. VII, 9, Nisi credideritis, non intelligetis.* In the body of the homily he adopts a dialogue with a rhetorical opponent who argues, "I understand that I may believe," while Augustine argues the reverse: "I believe that I may understand." To settle the debate he calls for an authoritative judge. Disqualifying literary figures, he turns to the prophet Isaiah and to this text. It is of no slight interest that this renowned Augustinian principle, on which Anselm based his *Proslogion: Faith Seeking Understanding,* arose from the African reading and translation of the Greek Bible. But as Quodvultdeus (and doubtless, Augustine) quickly adds, "let us merit to see what we believe," indicating that believing leads to desiring to see God.

8. The reference is to the megalithic religion entrenched among the Libyan tribes that inhabited the steppes and high plains south and west of Carthage, for which see the introduction (under "Religious Turmoil: Pagans and Paganism"). Although the origins lie in the Stone Age, megalithic religion proved to be a living cultural force not only in western Europe but also in North Africa well into Greco-Roman antiquity. The collections of the Bardo Museum in Tunis contain many examples of what Quodvultdeus had in mind. For an account, see M'hamed Fantar, *Le Bardo: Un palais, un musée* (Tunis: Alif, n.d.), 47–69. For the customs of worship, see "Megalithic Religions," *ER* 9:336–46. For discussion of the paganism of Carthage and its territories, see Serge Lancel, *Carthage: A History,* tr. Antonia Nevill (Oxford: Blackwell, 1995), 193–256.

9. Quodvultdeus's primary concern in this homily is the *Arriani*, as is obvious from his extended treatment above in *De symb.* 1.3–4.38 (CCL 60.305–17) and notes; see also the introduction (under "Religious Turmoil: Heretics").

10. The reference is to the Greco-Roman pagan religions, which persisted, indeed flourished, in Roman North Africa in Quodvultdeus's time, for which see the introduction (under "Religious Turmoil: Pagans and Paganism").

11. In what follows, Quodvultdeus seems to have been inspired by Augustine's account of his vision at Ostia (*Conf.* 9.10.24–25 [O'Donnell 1:113–14]), and by the confessional conversation with God (10.6 [O'Donnell 1:122]). Perhaps he is continuing here the Augustinian idea of faith leading to seeing God, in this case, face to face.

12. The image—darkness as punishment—evokes night as a time of fear and a time of trouble, even troubled sleep.

13. Ancient Carthage lay astride the shipping lanes of the Mediterranean, which made it a strategic and prosperous shipping center, long the rival of Rome and then one of Rome's prized possessions. Among the city's great distinctions were her harbors, especially her Punic ports, and her military harbor with Admiral's Island at its center. A maritime museum now stands on the outer peninsula, displaying its remarkable port facilities. Little wonder then that Quodvultdeus avails himself of this rather complex impersonation. Not only would his nautically minded audience have grasped his point right away, but also sailors, ship masters, and owners likely would have been among his hearers.

14. The allusion is to Adam in paradise before the Fall, and the comparison, borrowed from Psalm 48, is to Adam after the Fall.

15. See the introduction (under "Religious Turmoil: Pagans and Paganism"). The champion deity of North African paganism was Saturn, to whom the Phoenician god Baal Hammon was assimilated. Although a fertility god, Saturn-Baal, who absorbed many of Jupiter's (Jove's) characteristics, was nonetheless ruthless in the sacrifices he exacted. Indeed, in 1922, the Tophet (a sacred fire-burning pit) of archaic Carthage was first discovered. Subsequent excavation has revealed urns containing the calcinated bones of young children offered in sacrifice. For full discussion of the find, see Lancel, *Carthage*, 228–56. Juno, divine consort of Baal-Saturn, was supreme in Carthage; she was assimilated to the Phoenician goddess Tanit, known as the "face of Baal," who also survived as Caelestis. In whatever guise, however, she was the fertility goddess of rank. The third divinity of rank was Minerva, goddess of wisdom, who does not appear to have a Carthaginian incarnation, save that Jupiter, Juno, and Minerva—the Capitoline triad—became the symbol of Rome. The great imperially founded cities of second- and third-century North Africa like Dougga and Thuburbo Majus were dominated by

temples dedicated to the Capitoline triad. Mars had no prominence in Carthage in our period, whereas Venus was assimilated to Caelestis/ Tanit/Juno. The mention of other "monstrosities" *(portena)* is very likely a reference to statues carried in the processions of the public festivals and found in municipal statuary. But see above, *De symb.* 1.1.11–14 (CCL 60.306) and notes.

16. It is no surprise that Quodvultdeus starts his christological instruction as he does, for his most celebrated work, *Liber promissionum,* is animated by the thesis that sacred history is the progressive realization of the divine promises and prophecies. For the text, see CCL 60.11–189.

17. See the introduction (under "Religious Turmoil: The Jews and Judaism") and *De symb.* 1.5.1–19 (CCL 60.317–19) and notes, for what follows throughout chapter 4. On promise fulfillment, see the introduction (under "The Scriptures").

18. The phrase is *ab originale peccato.* Tertullian was the first Latin writer to address himself to the problem of original sin: He used *vitium originis* to describe the effect of the Fall on human nature (*De anima* 41 [CSEL 20.368]). The development of the doctrine took place in the Latin tradition, where it reached its climax; G. M. Lukken traces the development in *Original Sin in the Roman Liturgy: Research into the Theology of Original Sin in the Roman Sacramentaria and the Early Baptismal Liturgy* (Leiden: Brill, 1973), 266–96; for discussion of the African climate and development of the controversy, see Gerald Bonner, *St. Augustine of Hippo: Life and Controversies* (Philadelphia: Westminster, 1963), 312–93. For the history of the doctrine, see Henri Rondet, *Original Sin: The Patristic and Theological Background,* tr. C. Finegan (Staten Island: Alba House, 1972); and Paul Rigby, "Original Sin," *ATAE* 607–15.

19. The Adam-Christ topology, which follows, entered Christian tradition through Paul. As Quodvultdeus develops the parallel (recapitulation), it appears first in Irenaeus, *Adv. haer.* 5.14.2; 18.1.7; 21.1–2; 34.1. For a survey of the argument in early Christianity, see Robert L. Wilken, *Judaism and the Early Christian Mind: A Study of Cyril of Alexandria's Exegesis and Theology* (New Haven: Yale University Press, 1971), 93–143. For patristic texts, see Jean Daniélou, *From Shadows to Reality: Studies in the Biblical Typology of the Fathers,* tr. Wulstan Hibberd (London: Burns and Oates, 1960).

20. The apple as a poisonous drink is a theme found in several hymns of Ephrem the Syrian (c. 307–373): Among the effects of Satan's seduction of Eve is the fact that Adam became proud and presumptuous, specifically, that he was intoxicated by pride. Ephrem juxtaposes Adam's intoxication and that of Noah (Gen 9:20–29), who, after coming out of the ark, planted vineyards, drank of their fruit to the point of drunkenness and lay naked inside his tent. His youngest son, Ham, father of Canaan, saw him naked and is cursed for so dishonoring his father. See Tryggve Kronholm, *Motifs from*

Genesis 1–11 in the Genuine Hymns of Ephrem the Syrian: With Particular Reference to the Influence of Jewish Exegetical Tradition, Coniectanea Biblica–Old Testament Series 11 (Lund: Gleerup, 1978), 102–4 and n. 47. The theme is found also in rabbinic sources, where agreement is cited that the tree from which the first Adam ate was a vine. Intertwined is the theme that the poison is Satan's venom. Quodvultdeus is clearly an heir of this tradition.

21. For Quodvultdeus's earlier treatment of the church and Mary as mother and virgin, see above *De symb.* 1.1.1–4; 1.5.1–10 (CCL 60.305, 317–18) and notes. The image of the church as bride of Christ takes its origin in Eph 5:28–33. See Joseph C. Plumpe, *Mater Ecclesia: An Inquiry into the Concept of the Church as Mother in Early Christianity,* SCA 5 (Washington, DC: Catholic University of America Press, 1943). The virginal birth of the catechumen in the baptismal font became a fundamental baptismal theme in the Church Fathers and patristic liturgy both Eastern and Western. The texts are well collected and analyzed in Walter Bedard, *The Symbolism of the Baptismal Font in Early Christian Thought,* SST n.s. 45 (Washington: Catholic University of America Press, 1951), 45. For some striking developments in the newly discovered instructions of Chrysostom, see Finn, *Liturgy of Baptism,* 162–65; for Syriac Christianity, see T. M. Finn, *Early Christian Baptism and the Catechumenate: Italy, North Africa, and Egypt,* MF 5 (Collegeville, MN: Liturgical Press, 1992), 150–60; and idem, *From Death to Rebirth: Ritual and Conversion in Antiquity* (Mahwah, NJ: Paulist Press, 1997), 254–56.

22. For the Jews as "Christ-killers," starting with Herod and the Innocents, see the introduction (under "Religous Turmoil: The Jews and Judaism") and *De symb.* 1. 5.10–19 (CCL 60.318–19) and notes.

23. Death as sleep has a long and venerable history, which sees the boundary between life and death as permeable. The idea receives its Christian impetus in the gospel account of Jesus' healing the daughter of Jairus (Mark 5:39). See Alfred C. Rush, *Death and Burial in Christian Antiquity,* SCA 1 (Washington, DC: Catholic University of America Press, 1941), 1–22.

24. Quodvultdeus has conflated Christ's death, the Last Supper, and the Eucharist. Since the early second century the Eucharist was considered the "medicine of immortality" (Ignatius, *Letter to the Ephesians* 20.2). Very likely the homilist had in mind also the text of Gen 3:6–7, the temptation of Eve, when he speaks of the apple as a poisonous drink (above 4.26). Below in *De symb.* 3.1.10 (CCL 60:350), which deals with the rite of renunciation, Quodvultdeus says about the devil: "He promised him [Adam/Eve] immortality, and he gave him sin to drink." The extended medical metaphor in these passages (physician, court physician, poison, antidote) reflects the theme of the "medicine of immortality," rooted in the account of the goddess Isis's invention of the antidote for the poison of mortality, an image widespread in the Mediterranean world. The antidote was called *anathasia,* for a discussion of which, see William Schoedel, *Ignatius of Antioch: A Commentary*

on the Letters of Saint Ignatius of Antioch, Hermeneia (Philadelphia: Fortress, 1985), 95–98. None of the variants of the *Vetus Latina* indicates that anything other than fruit *(fructus)* and eating *(comedo/manduco)* was involved. For the initial statement of the theme, see above *De symb.* 2.4.26 (CCL 60.340) and note.

25. Implicit in the comparison is the baptismal font as the tomb for the Christian competents and also the womb. But see above, *De symb.* 2.4.6 (CCL 60.339) and 1.5.1–19 (CCL 60.317-19) and notes. But, in addition, the doctrine of Mary's virginity *in partu* is reflected: The argument—one from "fittingness" as Quodvultdeus here states—is that just as Christ came out of the tomb without removing the stone that sealed the tomb, he came forth from Mary's womb without breaking "the seals of her virginity" (Ambrose, *Ep.* 63.33 [PL 16:1198]); see also Michael O'Carroll, "Virginity of Mary, Virginity in Partu," *Theotokos,* 361-62. The parallels are virgin birth (incarnation) and rebirth (resurrection). As Quodvultdeus has been at pains to show, the competents will be reborn to resurrection-life from the virginal womb of the baptismal font.

26. The primary reference is to Tyconius (300–390), the revered and celebrated Donatist biblical interpreter, and to his *Liber Regularum* on interpretation, esecially on how the prophets and the typology testify to the New Testament. What follows is Quodvultdeus's discussion of how one counts the three days and nights in the tomb. It is important to note that some include as the first night the darkness that fell at Christ's crucifixion (Mark 15:33). For Tyconius's treatment, see William S. Babcock, ed., *Tyconius: The Book of Rules* (Atlanta: Scholars Press, 1989), 90–93 (the text used is F. C. Burkitt, ed., *The Rules of Tyconius,* Texts and Studies 3 [repr., Cambridge: Cambridge University Press, 1967]). The rule in question is V *(De temporibus),* which sets forth Tyconius's proposal (56–57). The work was written about 380, and Augustine addressed himself to it (Rule VII) in *Doctr. chr.* 3.30-37 (PL 34.88; CCL 32.102-16). See also Pamela Bright, *The Book of Rules of Tyconius: Its Purpose and Inner Logic,* Christianity and Judaism in Antiquity 2 (Notre Dame, IN: University of Notre Dame Press, 1988), esp. 159–90.

27. Thus, Tyconius, *Regula quinta* (Babcock ed.). The counting is inclusive: the day starts at sunset and runs to sunset.

28. The text is close to but not exactly the same as those given in *Vetus Itala* (Jülicher ed.): *oportet esse* are Quodvultdeus's words, but are not found in the others. The inclusion of noon is based on the Marcan account of the crucifixion (Mark 15:33): darkness covered the earth from midday to the ninth hour (3:00 P.M.).

29. The first North African to speak of "spiritual" interpretation was Tyconius, whose rejection of the literalistic, millenarian interpretation of scripture, specifically, of the Apocalypse, coupled with his vigorous insistence on spiritual interpretation, turned the tide in favor of acceptance of the

Apocalypse in the West (Bright, *Book of Rules,* 25; Bright also holds that Augustine misunderstood Tyconius's hermeneutical theory). For Augustine on Tyconius and his rules, see *Doctr. chr.* 3.33.46–37.56 (PL 34:83–90; CCL 32.105–16).

30. In this tripartite structure, Quodvultdeus seems to have in mind Rule III in Tyconius, "The Promises and the Law," although Tyconius does not use the terminology "before the law, under the law, and under grace." One need only recall that the structure of Quodvultdeus's *Liber promissionum* is *Ante legem, Sub lege, Sub gratia* (CCL 60.11, 68, 156). See the introduction (under "The Scriptures").

31. The Braun text reads *putet* (CCL 60.343), but an alternate reading is *pudet,* which seems preferable and is followed here.

32. Quodvultdeus's definition of omnipresence here is *ubique esse totum,* which echoes Augustine in the *Confessions* (1:3: *an ubique totus es et res nulla te totum capit?* [O'Donnell 1:4]), which in turn echoes Plotinus on the omnipresence of being (see *Enn.* 5:5.9; 6:4–5). I have continued the idea— whole and entire—although in the rest of this verse Quodvultdeus uses only *totus* without *ubique.*

33. Quodvultdeus echoes the *Confessions* here as well. In the seventh book Augustine records his break with Manichean thought, wherein he imagined that a large thing such as an elephant possessed more of God than a smaller thing such as a sparrow (7.1.2 [O'Donnell 1:74]). It is at this point that Augustine discovers Plotinus.

34. Quodvultdeus's terminology about the "Man-Assumed" *(homo susceptus)* reflects the usual way of speaking about the union of humanity and divinity in Christ *(homo assumptus)* in the fifth century. It reflects the discussions and debates that led from the Council of Ephesus (431) and to the Council of Chalcedon (451) and Dyophysite split, often called Nestorian. The mentor of the movement was Theodore of Mopsuestia (c. 350–428), who, as a member of the Antiochene school, sought to give the maximum value to the humanity the Son assumed. See M. Simonetti, "Theodore of Mopusestia," *EEC* 2824–25.

35. Quodvultdeus here reflects Augustine's insistence that Father, Son, and Spirit are inseparable because of subsistence, yet distinct because of their relations as persons. Although one in every aspect of substance (as Quodvultdeus here enumerates: eternity, majesty, and power), they are three, distinct as persons. Thus, for Quodvultdeus the Father is not the Son, nor the Son the Father, nor the Spirit either Father or Son. Nonetheless, all three persons are present, distinctively so. Or to put the matter as Western theology came to speak, the three Persons have a mutual immanence or penetration, that is, *circuminsessio.* The counterpart in the East was *perichoresis,* which emerged among the Cappadocians to designate the mutual immanence and

interpenetration of the divine and human natures in Christ. See A. Chollet, "Circumincession," *DTC* 2/2:2527–32.

36. In *De symb.* 1.9.6 (CCL 60.326), Quodvultdeus's concern is the Homoian Arianism that came from Italy with both Goths and refugees. Here in the simplest terms he is presenting received African teaching about the double procession of the Holy Spirit, a doctrine of which Augustine is the architect (*De trin.* 15.45–48). For extended patristic treatments, see Stanley M. Burgess, *The Holy Spirit: Ancient Christian Traditions* (Peabody, MA: Hendrickson, 1984), esp. 179–92; and his *The Holy Spirit: Eastern Christian Traditions* (Peabody, MA: Hendrickson, 1989), introduction. The Creed of Constantinople (381) professed belief "in the Holy Spirit, the Lord, the Giver of Life, who proceeds from the Father, who together with the Father and the Son is adored and glorified." Western versions even today speak of procession from the Father and the Son *[a patre et filioque]*. Double procession first appeared in the Council of Braga (675), a part of anti-Priscillianist tradition in Spain, and was accepted at Rome in the early eleventh century. It quickly became a major theological issue in the split between Christian East and West (as it remains today). For a history of the question and an Orthodox view, see Aristeides Papadakis, *Crisis in Byzantium: The Filioque Controversy in the Patriarchate of Gregory II of Cyprus (1283–1289)* (Crestwood, NY: St. Vladimir's Seminary Press, 1997).

37. Quodvultdeus recapitulates his Augustinian point that God, by his essence or substance, is totally present everywhere *(totus ubique)*. Thus, all of God is present to and with everything, but only to the extent that everything is present and with him. In those under grace, God indwells—grace enables it. In Christ the fullness of the Trinity dwelled entire in itself (*in se ipso* [*Ep.* 187.6.18 (CSEL 57.96)]). Thus, one does not say that the Son suffered for humankind without meaning that the passion was the work of the Father, of the Son, and of the Holy Spirit. For discussion of Augustine's doctrine of the divine presence, see his *Ep.* 187 (ibid.) *(Ad Dard),* and Eugene TeSelle, *Augustine the Theologian* (London: Burns and Oates, 1970), 152–56.

38. See *De symb.* 1.9.1–30 (CCL 60.326–29), where he takes up what the Arians were asserting about the Holy Spirit and develops his refutation; see also the introduction (under "Religious Turmoil: Heretics").

39. The second infancy is baptism. On grace as prevenient, Quodvultdeus is clearly following his mentor Augustine, who, although he once thought that faith was "in us from ourselves," held clearly that faith "was preceded by God's grace" (*De praedestinatione sanctorum* 3.7 [PL 44.964]). For a valuable collection of texts on grace in Augustine, see J. Patout Burns, ed., *Theological Anthropology*, Sources of Early Christian Thought (Philadelphia: Fortress Press, 1981), 12–22 (discussion) and 61–108 (texts), esp. 96–108 (he does not include *De praed. sanct.*).

40. Quodvultdeus has grain primarily in view, perhaps both wheat and corn. In any case, at his time North Africa, along with Egypt, was Rome's granary, largely because of the fertile coastal plain (called the *Sahel* in modern Tunisia) that ran from Libya along the Mediterranean to Mauritania. The soil was "light" and best suited then, as now, for growing grain, fruits, grapes, and olives. Quodvultdeus's audience would clearly respond to the Pauline imagery.

41. For the classic statement of this theme, see Quodvultdeus's ancient predecessor, Cyprian (*De eccl.* 6–7, 14, 23, 25 [CSEL 3/1.204–33]); Maurice Bévenot, ed., *The Lapsed: The Unity of the Catholic Church,* ACW 25 (New York: Paulist Press, 1956), 5–8, 48–50, 56–57, 64, 67–68, especially his celebrated dictum that one cannot have God for one's Father if one does not have not the church for her or his mother (p. 6).

42. The reference is to the Eucharist, to which the competents may now aspire and to which they will process immediately after baptism as new members of their new family.

THE THIRD HOMILY ON THE CREED

1. Quodvultdeus's reference is to the rite of entry, inscription, which involved exorcism, the imposition of hands, the sign of the cross, and the ingestion of salt. It marked the entry to the catechumenate whether the candidate was an infant, a teenager, or an adult. From that time the candidate was thought to be in the womb of the church. For the image of the church as mother, see below, *De symb.* 3.13.1–7 (CCL 60.363) and note; Joseph C. Plumpe, *Mater Ecclesia: An Inquiry into the Concept of the Church as Mother in Early Christianity,* SCA 5 (Washington, DC: Catholic University of America Press, 1943).

2. See above, *De symb.* 1.1.2–5 (CCL 60.305). The parallel evoked is rooted in the Pauline doctrine of the "two-Adams" (Rom 13:10; Eph 1:10) and is developed in detail by Irenaeus in both *Demonstration of the Apostolic Teaching* and *Against the Heresies.* Quodvultdeus's Christology was built around the theory of recapitulation *(anakephalaiôsis),* which some consider the most important early Christian contribution to theology. He writes:

> ...when he became incarnate and was made man, he recapitulated in himself the long history of man, and summing up and giving us salvation in order that we might receive again in Christ Jesus what we had lost in Adam, that is, the image and likeness of God (*Adv. haer.* 3.18.1 [tr. J. Quasten, *Patrology,* vol. 1, Westminister: the Newman Press, 1950, 296]; see also 3.17.1; 5.14.2; 5.19.1; 5.21.5; see also Dem. 7.31, 39–40, 55 (tr. J. Smith,

St. Irenaeus: Proof of the Apostolic Preaching, ACW 16, New York:
Newman Press/Paulist Press, 1952]).

God formed Adam out of dust to be head of the world and to pass on
his nature constituted in grace. But Adam lost this for himself and his
descendants. God, therefore, formed flesh and blood from Mary for his son
to renew and restore his original plan. Christ became the new head, from
whom all the sons and daughters of Adam would have a new life and nature.
Mary, thus, is the new Eve. For a treatment of the theory in Irenaeus, see
Jean Daniélou, *Gospel Message and Hellenistic Culture,* tr. J. A. Baker
(Philadelphia: Westminster Press, 1977), 166–83.

    3. Quodvultdeus refers to the rites of the previous evening's vigil—
the scrutiny—which involved scrutiny, renunciation of Satan, and *redditio
symboli.* See above, *De symb.* 1.1.4–8 and 2.2.1–2 (CCL 60.305, 335), and the
introduction (under "The Pivotal Rites").

    4. Quodvultdeus seems to have in mind the ingestion of a pharma-
cological poison for abortion, for which see Aline Roussell, *Porneia: On
Desire and the Body in Antiquity,* tr. Felicia Pheasant (Oxford: Basil Blackwell,
1988), 44–46; but see below, *De symb.* 1:10 (CCL 60.350) and n. 7.

    5. Although Revelation 12 has parallels in the Hebrew Bible and
other Jewish literature, the closest parallel to this section is the Greco-
Roman version of Apollo's birth. Leto had become pregnant by Zeus. The
dragon Python foresaw that this child, a son—Apollo—would replace him as
the ruler over the oracle of Delphi, and so he sought to kill the child at birth.
Apollo slew the dragon. See Adela Yarbro Collins, *The Combat Myth in the
Book of Revelation,* HDS 9 (Missoula, MT: Scholars Press, 1976), 61–70.
Quodvultdeus will come back to this allusion at the end of this homily
(13.4–7 [CCL 60.363] and note).

    6. Although Mary's preservation of virginity in the bearing of Jesus
(virginitas in partu) first appears in the Apocrypha (*Protoevangium of James*
19-20; *Odes of Solomon* 19), Zeno of Verona (d. 375) seems to be the first of
the Fathers to make it explicit in the West: "O great mystery! Mary, an incorrupt virgin conceived, after conception she brought forth as a virgin, after
childbirth she remained a virgin" (*Tractatus* 2 [PL 11:415; CCL
22.145-204]). Clearly, however, it comes to Quodvultdeus from Augustine,
who says: "She had conceived without male seed, brought forth without corruption, retained her integrity after childbirth" (*Serm.* 215.3 [PL 38:1073]).
But see above, *De symb.* 1.5.6-19 (CCL 60.317-18) and 2.4.1-7 (CCL
60.338-39) and notes.

    7. Quodvultdeus's word is *propinavit,* which evokes the image of hail-
ing one with a drink in one's hand, which in turn would evoke the image
above. See n. 4, and *De symb.* 1.4.25-26 (CCL 60.315): Satan's venom as a
drink, sin, and the contrast between Eve and Mary. But what follows suggests
that the renunciation is a nullification of the promise and pledge.

8. For the spectacles and what follows, see the introduction (under "Religious Turmoil: Pagans and Paganism"), and Quodvultdeus's extensive discussion above, *De symb.* 1.1.17–2:28 (CCL 60.306–10) and notes.

9. The Vulgate text reads: *oculi domini super justos et aures eius preces eorum.* The entire sentence, however, evokes Heb 4:12–13, which may explain the divergence between the Vulgate and Quodvultdeus's citation of the psalm. On the other hand, as noted in the introduction (under "The Scriptures"), there is much evidence throughout the creedal homilies that his version of the Bible is not the Vulgate. One must bear in mind, however, that Quodvultdeus cites from memory, has an amanuensis, and tailors his citations to his point, as noted in the introduction (under "The Scriptures").

10. The phrase is *circumscripsimus membra,* which means in the context that we are circumscribed by our bodily members. When God "circumscripts" them, he is not circumscribed thereby. For a more expansive statement of God's essential and uncircumscribed presence everywhere and entire, see above, *De symb.* 2.7.1–5, 9.1–12 (CCL 60.344–47) and notes. In 2.7, Quodvultdeus addresses God's being everywhere whole and entire in the incarnation; in 2.9, his principal concern is circumincession. In any case, he shows himself a disciple of Augustine, as the notes document.

11. Quodvultdeus has cited the verse only partially, tailoring it to his point (see n. 9 above). The Vulgate reads: *si caelum et caeli caelorum non te capiunt quanto magis domus ista quem aedificavi....*

12. Here again, Quodvultdeus isolates a biblical verse, this time from Paul. The entire verse is a patchwork of sayings from the Bible (2 Sam 7:8–14; Isa 43:6; Jer 31:9), and some think that the passage is an intercalation in 2 Corinthians.

13. Still another instance of Quodvultdeus's adaptive use of scripture—he seems to have intercalated 1 Cor 13:12 *(videmus nunc per speculum en enigmate ...)* into Exodus, for the Vulgate reads: loquebatur autem Dominus ad Moses facie ad faciem sicut loqui sole homo ad amicum suum.

14. The Vulgate does not identify the mount.

15. The sentence is difficult, because it compresses in few words the doctrine of mystical (spiritual and allegorical are synonymous with mystical) interpretation. As noted in the introduction, toward the end of his life Quodvultdeus devoted the longest and most influential work, *Liber promissionum,* to biblical interpretation. He intended it to be a handbook for preachers. In the process it became an important vehicle that made Augustininan biblical interpretation accessible to future generations of preachers. For Augustine's treatment of interpretation, see his *De doctrina christiana,* especially the third book (3:10–29 on literal and figurative interpretation), which Quodvultdeus appropriates here. For discussion, see *De Doctrina Christiana: A Classic of Western Culture,* ed. Duane W. H. Arnold and Pamela Bright, Christianity and Judaism in Antiquity 9 (Notre Dame, IN: University of Notre

Dame Press, 1995), especially Roland Teske, "Criteria for Figurative Interpretation in St. Augustine," 109–22. For Augustine, the "temporal reality" is the source of the discovery of the eternal meaning intended by the author, who is ultimately the Holy Spirit. By "mystical figures" Quodvultdeus appears to mean what Augustine meant by "figures of things": they either symbolize or prefigure something else. Quodvultdeus is about to identify the *veritas manifesta* typologically, citing 1 Cor 10:3–4 and Gal 4:4.

16. Quodvultdeus's verb form for the self-actuation of the divine in the incarnation is *infunderet se,* and, in using it, he is guided by the biblical account of the annunciation, which describes the Holy Spirit overshadowing Mary (*uper veniet in te* [Luke 1:35]), or that what is to be born of Mary is the result of infusion of the Holy Spirit (*quod ... in ea natum est de Spiritu Sancto est* [Matt 1:20]). Zeno of Verona (d. 375), in addressing himself to this delicate topic, seems to prefer the Lucan emphasis, for he speaks of the Word entering Mary's body first though her ear (*Hom.* 1.3.19). For Quodvultdeus's concern about teaching that Mary's virginity remained intact, see above, *De symb.* 1.5.1–10 and 2.6.1–7 (CCL 60.317, 342–43) and notes.

17. In paralleling the two births—generation and incarnation—Quodvultdeus has in mind the Arians, who occupy his attention above in *De symb.* 1.3.9–4.6 (CCL 60.311–13) and notes; see also the introduction (under "Religious Turmoil: Heretics").

18. Quodvultdeus here is adverting to angelic virginity. For an analysis of the Fathers on the angels and their role in the mysteries of redemption, see Jean Daniélou, *The Angels and Their Mission* (Westminster, MD: Newman Press, 1956). For Mary's virginity and the virgin birth, see above, *De symb.* 1.5.4–9 (CCL 60.317–18) and 2.4.24–28 (CCL 60.340–41).

19. See also below, 5.13–24 (CCL 60.357) of this homily: These passages taken together are a recapitulation of the anti-Judaism that Quodvultdeus develops extensively above in *De symb.* 1.5.13–15 (CCL 60.319) and 2.5.1–3 (CCL 60.335–36) and notes; see also the introduction (under "Religious Turmoil: The Jews and Judaism").

20. By using *obligatos,* Quodvultdeus seems to be thinking of the bondage of the law. For the Magi–Herod contrast, see above, *De symb.* 2.4.8–23 (CCL 60.339–40).

21. Although Quodvultdeus's directly intended audience is competents (see the introduction under "The Audience"), members of the faithful were clearly present, including nuns, the *virgines* here recognized.

22. The Latin *vexillum nostrum* and what follows reflect an understanding of the passion that became standard in the early medieval church—the life of Christ and Christian life as combat—inspiring the celebrated hymn of Venantius Fortunatus (540–600), chaplain to the monastery of Holy Cross, poet and finally bishop of Poitiers (600). The incipit is: *Vexilla regis prodeunt, fulget crucis mysterium....* For the full text, see F. J. E. Raby, *A History of*

Christian-Latin Poetry from the Beginnings to the Close of the Middle Ages, 2nd ed. (Oxford: Clarendon Press, 1953), 89–90.

23. Quodvultdeus's statement reflects the foundation of early christological thinking—the Son of God became the Son of Man that the sons of men might become the sons of God. First formulated by Irenaeus of Lyons (*Adv. haer.* 3.18.6–7; 5.1.1), this assumptive union came by the fourth century to be called *theôsis*/deification. For discussion of the patristic development, see H.-I. Dalmais, "Divinisation, Patristique grecque," DS 3:1376–89; for a contemporary Orthodox view, see Panayiotis Nellas, *Deification in Christ: The Nature of the Human Person,* tr. Norman Russell (Crestwood, NY: St. Vladimir's Seminary Press, 1997). For Quodvultdeus's audience, deification begins with baptismal rebirth.

24. The operative term in the clause is *spectaculum,* which Quodvultdeus elsewhere uses for the theater, circus, and the amphitheater. The combat theme that dominates this section (3.5.1–12) is dealt with extensively above; see *De symb.* 1.2.1–28 (CCL 60.307–10) and notes. Perhaps he is invoking for the audience the mock battles staged in the Carthage amphitheater.

25. For Quodvultdeus's other depictions of the Jews, see the introduction (under "Religious Turmoil: The Jews and Judaism"), and *De symb.* 3.4.10–18 (CCL 60.354–55), 1.5.13–15 (CCL 60.353), 2.5.13–19; 6.7–15 (CCL 60.318, 342–44) and notes.

26. Quodvultdeus seems to be paraphrasing the Johannine account of Jesus' arrest, though he adheres fairly closely to the wording of the Vulgate.

27. Acts speaks of the "upper room" located within the walls of Jerusalem and revered among early Christians as the mother church. About the year 130 a small chapel had been erected on the traditional site of the Last Supper. Between 335 and 347 it was enlarged with a basilica called the Upper Church of the Apostles and the Church of Sion. The church was one of six fourth-century churches in Jerusalem that played leading roles in the Holy Week liturgy recorded by the western pilgrim Egeria in her celebrated diary, for which see George E. Gingras, ed. and tr., *Egeria: Diary of a Pilgrimage,* ACW 38 (New York: Newman/Paulist Press, 1970), esp. 24-26 and nn. 107, 108, 117; see now also John Wilkinson, ed., *Egeria's Travels,* rev. 3rd ed. (Warminster: Aris and Phillips, 1999). Quodvultdeus emphasizes "one" house to signify the reunification of the terrified and scattered disciples mentioned in the previous verse (22).

28. Quodvultdeus here is employing exegetical terms (*praedicta, promissa, impleta*), which he will systematize in *Liber promissionum* composed in Naples at the end of his life as a manual for preachers (CCL 60.1–223). The work had a deep influence on medieval biblical interpretation, its inspiration being North African biblical interpretation shaped especially by Augustine's *De doctrina christiana* (for a recent discussion, see Roland Teske,

"Criteria for Figurative Interpretation in St. Augustine,"in *De Doctrina Christiana: A Classic of Western Culture*, ed. Duane W. H. Arnold and Pamela Bright, *De Doctrina Christiana: A Western Classic*, 109–22. The work is a systematic collection of biblical testimonies to the promises and prophecies that single out the events on which the history of salvation turns as if on an axis, achieving fulfillment in Christ and the church at the end of time. The work is divided into three parts. The first, *Liber promissionum*, collects prefigurations of the kingdom to come; the second, *Dimidium temporis*, prophesies about the end of time, focusing on the "last day"; the third, *Gloria sanctorum*, concentrates on the fulfillment of the promises and prophecies. For discussion of the *Liber*, see René Braun, *Opera Quodvultdeo Carthaginiensi episcopo tributa*, CCL 60 (Turnholt: Brepols, 1976), vi–l; and Daniel G. Van Slyke, "Quodvultdeus of Carthage: Political Change and Apocalyptic Theology in the Fifth-Century Roman Empire" (Ph.D. diss., St. Louis University, 2001).

29. The Vulgate text is quite different: *vivicabit nos post duos dies in die tertia suscitabit nos et vivemus in conspectu eius.*

30. Quodvultdeus employs allegory to make what is a typological point, in that he sets out a series of exact and detailed comparisons.

31. The term *transitus* here seems to refer to the passage of Christ from life to death and from death to life. Arising in the east (Egypt? Syria?), the term is used in the fifth and subsequent centuries to refer to the apocryphal accounts of the death of Mary, specifically, her transition from earth to heaven. For a study of the early Christian literature on the *transitus*, see Walter J. Burghardt, *The Testimony of the Patristic Age Concerning Mary's Death* (Westminster, MD: Newman Press, 1961), 13–18.

32. The citation is quite different in the Vulgate: *et aspicient ad me quem confixerunt.*

33. That Quodvultdeus thinks the end is imminent is not surprising for two reasons. First, most of North Africa had fallen to the Vandals, and Carthage was under Vandal siege. Indeed, two siege homilies from Quodvultdeus are extant: *De tempore barbarico 1, 2* (CCL 60.421–37, 471–86). Second, apocalypticism was characteristic of North African Christianity, the first records of which are martyrdom accounts. One of the treasured books of North African Christians was Revelation. Although the oldest commentary is that of Victorinus of Pettau (d. 304), the most intriguing is that of Tyconius, the incisive North African Christian thinker who also wrote the first manual of biblical interpretation in the Latin West, *The Book of Rules*. Although Tyconius's commentary exists only in fragments and he does not appear to have been an apocalyptic, the fact that he wrote a commentary on Revelation suggests the importance of the work in North Africa. See K. Steinhauser, *The Apocalypse Commentary of Tyconius: A History of Its Reception and Influence* (Frankfurt: Peter Lang, 1987); Van Slyke, "Quodvultdeus of Carthage"; and Pamela Bright, *The Book of Rules of Tyconius: Its Purpose and*

Inner Logic, Christianity and Judaism in Antiquity 2 (Notre Dame, IN: University of Notre Dame Press, 1988).

34. See the introduction (under "Religious Turmoil: Heretics"), *De symb.* 2.9.1–12 (CCL 60.345–47) and 1.9.1–30 (CCL 60.326–29) and notes. In the latter passage, Quodvultdeus addresses himself in detail to the Homoians' doctrine of the Holy Spirit.

35. Quodvultdeus here reflects Augustine's theology of the Holy Spirit and his "psychological" explanation of the Trinity in this brief sentence: The Holy Spirit proceeds as love between the Father and the Son as the Gift (*De trin.* 14.6.5, 7). See Eugene TeSelle, "Holy Spirit," *ATAE* 434–37; and Augustino Trappé, "St Augustine," in *Patrology,* ed. A. Berardino, trans. P. Solari (Westminster: Christian Classics, 1987), 4:371–372, 428–30.

36. Quodvultdeus develops a similar refutation above in *De symb.* 1.4.23–26 (CCL 60.315).

37. Quodvultdeus has in mind Homoian Arians, who included the Vandals moving toward proconsular Africa to besiege and conquer Carthage (439) and the Gothic Roman troops, whose task was to keep the Donatists in line. In contrast to both, whom he locates in a "corner of the world" *(in angulo mundi),* is the *ecclesia catholica,* which is resident in the whole world.

38. The reference is to the Genesis account of Adam's creation and condemnation. The Vulgate reads that God formed Adam *de limo terrae* (Gen 2:7) and, when Adam and Eve sinned, that he condemned Adam *ut operetur terram de qua sumptus est* (Gen 3:23).

39. For the *vehiculum mortis,* see below, *De symb.* 3.11.5 (CCL 60.347), and above, 1.10.16 (CCL 60.331) and n. 73. Here and below in 11, Quodvultdeus evokes again the vision of Ezekiel (3:12) and Elijah's chariot of fire (2 Kgs 2:11) to speak about Christ's ascension and, for those in Christ, their own resurrection and ascension.

40. See Cyprian, *De eccl.* 6 (CSEL 3/2.214), from which this celebrated line is taken. At the outset of this homily (3.1.2; CCL 60.349) Quodvultdeus invokes the church as mother, which Cyprian uses frequently as he develops his doctrine of the necessity of the church, outside of which there is no salvation (*Ep.* 73.21 [CSEL 3/2.295]). Thus, Quodvultdeus speaks of the "boundaries." See also Cyprian, *De eccl.* 23 (CSEL 3/1.231), where he also speaks of the church as mother; and see Plumpe, *Mater Ecclesia.*

41. Quodvultdeus continues to follow Cyprian in his doctrine of the necessity of the church for salvation. In *De eccl.* 14 (CSEL 3/1.222–24), Cyprian argues that not even martyrdom can save one who is not in the church, not to mention the gifts of prophecy, exorcism, and miracles. Quodvultdeus has in mind heretics, especially those against whom he directed the homilies.

42. Quodvultdeus employs a striking wordplay: *delabata/dotata* (13.2) and *dote* (13.4), all in the context of the marriage contract. As bride, the

church, whitewashed *(delabata)*, is endowed *(dotata)* with Christ's blood and receives everything from the Bridegroom as her dowry *(dote)*. It is difficult to bring out in the translation that Christ's red blood whitewashes the church, which, in this translator's view is part of Quodvultdeus's imagery. But see above, *De symb.* 1.6.1–14 (CCL 60.320–21) and notes, esp. n. 49 on Quodvultdeus's stiking image of the cross as Christ's marriage bed.

43. Quodvultdeus's settled view of heresy is that it sets the group or congregation "apart from the whole world and [confines them] to a corner of the whole world" (above 3.9.9 [CCL 60.361]). But see n. 37 above. For him, heretics like the Arians, so much in his mind, are the very opposite of Catholic. To paraphrase a now celebrated political axiom: Just as all politics is local, so all heresy is local.

44. Beginning with Revelation's image of the woman "who had given birth to the male child" and was pursued by the serpent into the wilderness and pressed by the dragon (Rev 12:13–17), Mary, Eve, and the church were perceived as transparencies each of the other: Eve as the mother of God's new race, Mary as the mother of God, and the Church as the mother of the living. In opening this third homily (1.1–6) by citing the church as mother of the living, Quodvultdeus seems to be reflecting Augustine, who wrote:

> As Mary gave birth to him who is your head, so the church gives
> birth to you. For the Church also is both mother and virgin:
> mother in the womb of our love, virgin in her inviolate faith.
> She is the mother of many nations who are yet one body and are
> thus likened to that one Virgin Mary, the mother of many but
> yet of the one. (Augustine, *Serm.* 25.8, cited in Hugo Rahner,
> *Our Lady and the Church,* tr. Sebastian Bullock [New York:
> Pantheon, 1961], 5)

Rahner's study is a series of reflections on patristic views of Mary as *typos* of the church.

BIBLIOGRAPHY

Arnold, Duane W. H., and Pamela Bright, eds. *De Doctrina Christiana: A Western Classic.* Christianity and Judaism in Antiquity 9 (Notre Dame, IN: The University of Notre Dame Press, 1995).

Auguet, Roland. *Cruelty and Civilization: The Roman Games.* London: George Allen and Unwin, 1972.

Ayers, Lewis. "'Remember That You Are Catholic' (Serm. 52.2): Augustine on the Unity of the Triune God." *JEC* 8 (2000): 39–82.

Babcock, William S., ed. *Tyconius: The Book of Rules.* Atlanta: Scholars Press, 1989.

Barnes, Michel. "The Arians of Book V, and the Genre of De Trinitate." *JTS* n.s. 44 (1993): 185–95.

Barnes, Michel R., and Daniel H. Williams, eds. *Arianism after Arius: Essays on the Development of the Fourth Century Trinitarian Conflicts.* Edinburgh: T. & T. Clark, 1993.

Beacham, Richard C. *The Roman Theatre and Its Audience.* Cambridge, MA: Harvard University Press, 1992.

Bedard, Walter. *The Symbolism of the Baptismal Font in Early Christian Thought.* SST 45 ser. 2. Washington, DC: Catholic University of America Press, 1951.

Berardino, Angelo, ed. *Patrology,* vol. 4. Translated by P. Solari. Westminster, MD: Christian Classics, 1987.

Bévenot, Maurice, ed. *The Lapsed: The Unity of the Catholic Church.* ACW 25. New York: Paulist Press, 1956.

Boismard, M. E. "'I Renounce Satan, his Pomps, and his Works.'" In *Baptism in the New Testament: A Symposium,* translated by D. Askew, 107–14. Baltimore: Helicon, 1964.

Bomgardner, David. "An Analytic Study of North African Amphitheaters." Diss., University of Michigan, 1985.

Bonner, Gerald. *St. Augustine of Hippo: Life and Controversies.* Philadelphia: Westminster, 1963.

Boyd, William K. *The Edicts of the Theodosian Code.* 1905. Reprint, New York: AMS Press, 1969.

Braun, René. "Quodvultdeus." *DS* 15:2884–89.

Braun, René, ed. *Livre des promesses et des prédictions de Dieu.* SC 101, 102. Paris: Éditions du Cerf, 1964.

129

———. *Opera Quodvultdeo Carthaginiensi Episcopo Tributa*. CCL 60. Turnholt: Brepols, 1976.

Bright, Pamela. *The Book of Rules of Tyconius: Its Purpose and Inner Logic*. Christianity and Judaism in Antiquity 2. Notre Dame, IN: University of Notre Dame Press, 1988.

Bright, Pamela, ed. *Augustine and the Bible*. The Bible through the Ages 2. Notre Dame, IN: University of Notre Dame Press, 1999.

Burgess, Stanley M. *The Holy Spirit: Ancient Christian Traditions*. Peabody, MA: Hendrickson, 1984.

———. *The Holy Spirit: Eastern Christian Traditions*. Peabody, MA: Hendrickson, 1989.

Burghardt, Walter J. *The Testimony of the Patristic Age Concerning Mary's Death*. Westminster, MD: Newman Press, 1961.

Burns, J. Patout. "On Rebaptism: Social Organization in the Third Century Church." *JEC* 1 (1993): 367–403.

Burns, J. Patout, ed. *Theological Anthropology*. Sources of Early Christian Thought. Philadelphia: Fortress Press, 1981.

Busch, Benedict. "De initiatione christiana secundum sanctum Augustinum." *ELA* 52 (1938): 159–78, 385–483.

Chadwick, Henry. *Contra Celsum*. Cambridge: Cambridge University Press, 1965.

Chollet, A. "Circumincession," *DTC* 2.2:2527–32.

Christopher, Joseph P. *St. Augustine: The First Catechetical Instruction*. ACW 2. New York: Newman Press/Paulist Press, 1946.

Cohen, Jeremy. *Living Letters of the Law: Ideas of the Jew in Medieval Christianity*. Berkeley: University of California Press, 1999.

Collins, Adela Yarbro. *The Combat Myth in the Book of Revelation*. HDS 59. Missoula, MT: Scholars Press, 1976.

Dalmais, H.-I. "Divinisation, Patristique grecque." *DS* 3:1376–89.

Daniélou, Jean. *The Angels and Their Mission*. Westminster, MD: Newman Press, 1956.

———. *From Shadows to Reality: Studies in the Biblical Typology of the Fathers*. Translated by Wulstan Hibberd. London: Burns and Oates, 1960.

Davies, Roy W., David Breez, and Valerie A. Maxfield, eds. *Service in the Roman Army*. New York: Columbia University Press, 1989.

De Lange, N. R. M. *Origen and the Jews: Studies in Jewish-Christian Relations in Third-Century Palestine*. Cambridge: Cambridge University Press, 1976.

Dixon, Susanne. *The Roman Family*. Baltimore: Johns Hopkins University Press, 1992.

Dondeyne, A. "La discipline des scrutins dans l'Église latine avant Charlemagne." *RHE* 28 (1932): 5–33.

Driscoll, Michael S. "Penance in Transition: Popular Piety and Practice." In *Medieval Liturgy: A Book of Essays*, edited by Lizette Larson-Miller. New York: Garland, 1997.

Edwards, Mark J. "Neoplatonism." *ATAE* 588–91.

Fantar, M'Hamed. *Le Bardo: Un palais, un musée.* Tunis: Alif, n.d.

Finn, T. M. *Early Christian Baptism and the Catechumenate: Italy, North Africa, and Egypt.* MF 5. Collegeville, MN: Liturgical Press, 1992.

———. *From Death to Rebirth: Ritual and Conversion in Antiquity.* Mahwah, NJ: Paulist Press, 1997.

———. "It Happened One Saturday Night: Ritual and Conversion in Augustine's North Africa." *JAAR* 58 (1990): 589–616.

———. *The Liturgy of Baptism in the Baptismal Instructions of St. John Chrysostom.* SCA 15. Washington, DC: Catholic University of America Press, 1967.

———. "Ritual and Conversion: The Case of Augustine." In *Nova et Vetera: Patristic Studies in Honor of Thomas Patrick Halton*, 149–61. Washington, DC: Catholic University of America Press, 1998.

Fischer, Bonifatius, ed. *Vetus Latina: Die Reste Der Altlateinichen Bibel.* Freiburg: Herder, 1949–.

Fredriksen, Paula. "*Excaecati Occulta Justitia Dei:* Augustine on Jews and Judaism," *JEC* 3 (1995): 320–41.

Frend, W. H. C. *The Donatist Church: A Movement of Protest in Roman North Africa.* 3rd. ed. Oxford: Clarendon Press, 1987.

Gingras, George E., ed. and tr. *Egeria: Diary of a Pilgrimage.* ACW 38. New York: Newman Press/Paulist Press,1970.

Grillmeyer, Aloys. *Christ in Christian Tradition.* Volume 1, *From the Apostolic Age to Chalcedon (451).* Translated by John Bowden. Atlanta: John Knox Press, 1975.

Halm, C., ed. *Victoris Vitensis historia persecutionis Africanae provinciae sub Geiserico et Hunrico regibus Wandalorum.* Monumenta Germaniae Historica. Berlin, Weidmann, 1879.

Hanson, R. P. C. *The Search for the Christian Doctrine of God: The Arian Controversy 318–381.* Edinburgh: T. & T. Clark, 1988.

Harmless, William. *Augustine and the Catechumenate.* Collegeville, MN: Liturgical Press, 1995.

Humphrey, John H. *Roman Circuses: Arenas for Chariot Racing.* Berkeley: University of California Press, 1985.

Hunt, David. "Christianizing the Roman Empire." In *The Theodosian Code*, edited by Jill Harries and Ian Wood, 143–58. Ithaca, NY: Cornell University Press, 1993.

Jülicher, Adolf, ed. *Itala: Das Neue Testament in altlateinischer Überlieferung.* Berlin/New York: de Gruyter, 1972–.

Kopecek, Thomas A. *A History of Neo-Arianism.* 2 vols. Patristic Monograph Series 8. Cambridge, MA: Philadelphia Patristic Foundation, 1979.

Kronholm, Tryggve. *Motifs from Genesis 1–11 in the Genuine Hymns of Ephrem the Syrian: With Particular Reference to the Influence of Jewish Exegetical Tradition.* Coniectanea Biblica–Old Testament Series 11. Lund: Gleerup, 1978.

Lampe, G. W. H., ed. *The Cambridge History of the Bible.* Volume 2, *The West from the Fathers to the Reformation.* Cambridge: Cambridge University Press, 1969.

Lancel, Serge. *Carthage: A History.* Translated by Antonia Nevill. Oxford: Blackwell, 1995.

Larson-Miller, Lizette, ed. *Medieval Liturgy: A Book of Essays.* New York/London: Garland, 1997.

LeBohec, Yann. "Juifs et judaisants dans l'Afrique romaine: Remarques onomastiques." *Antiquités Africaines* 17 (1981): 209–29.

Leon, Harry J. *The Jews of Ancient Rome.* Rev. Ed., Carolyn Osiek. Peabody, MA: Hendrickson, 1995.

Leonard, John K. "Rites of Marriage in the Wesern Middle Ages." In *Medieval Liturgy: A Book of Essays,* edited by Lizette Larson-Miller, 165–202. New York/London: Garland, 1997.

Lukken, G. M. *Original Sin in the Roman Liturgy: Research into the Theology of Original Sin in the Roman Sacramentaria and the Early Baptismal Liturgy.* Leiden: Brill, 1973.

Maguire, Alban. *Blood and Water: The Wounded Side of Christ in Early Christian Literature.* SST 108. Washington, DC: Catholic University of America Press, 1958.

Maxfield, Valerie A. *Service in the Roman Army.* New York: Columbia University Press, 1989.

McHugh, Michael. "Quodvultdeus." *ATAE* 693–94.

Metzger, Bruce M. *The Early Versions of the New Testament.* Oxford: Clarendon Press, 1977.

Moorhead, John, tr. *Victor of Vita: History of the Vandal Persecution.* Liverpool: Liverpool University Press, 1992.

Morin, G. "Pour une future édition des opuscules de saint Quodvultdeus, évêque de cartage au Ve siècle." *Revue Bénédictine* 31 (1914):156–62.

Nellas, Panayiotis. *Deification in Christ: The Nature of the Human Person.* Translated by Norman Russell. Crestwood, NY: St. Vladimir's Seminary Press, 1997.

Norman, Naomi. "Excavations in the Circus at Carthage." *Archaeology* 40 (1987): 46–57.

O'Carroll, Michael. "Immaculate Conception." In *Theotokos,* 179–82.

———. "Virginity of Mary, Virginity in Partu." In *Theotokos,* 357–62.

O'Donnell, James J. "Bible." *ATAE* 99–102.

O'Donnell, James J., ed. *Augustine: Confessions I: Introduction and Text.* Oxford: Clarendon Press, 1992.

Papadakis, Aristeides. *Crisis in Byzantium: The Filioque Controversy in the Patriarchate of Gregory II of Cyprus (1283-1289)*. Crestwood, NY: St. Vladimir's Seminary Press, 1997.

Plass, Paul. *The Game of Death in Ancient Rome: Arena Sport and Political Suicide*. Madison: University of Wisconsin Press, 1995.

Plumpe, Joseph C. *Mater Ecclesia: An Inquiry into the Concept of Chruch as Mother in Early Christianity*. SCA 5. Washington, DC: The Catholic University of America Press, 1943.

Poque, Suzanne. *Augustin d'Hippone: Sermons pour la Pâque*. SC 116. Paris: Éditions du Cerf, 1966.

Poschmann, Bernhard. *Penance and the Anointing of the Sick*. Translated by Francis Courtney. New York: Herder and Herder, 1964.

Quasten, Johannes. "Theodore of Mopsuestia on the Exorcism of the Cilicium." *HTR* 5 (1942): 209-19.

Raby, F. J. E. *A History of Christian-Latin Poetry from the Beginnings to the Close of the Middle Ages*. 2nd ed. Oxford: Clarendon Press, 1953.

Rahner, Hugo. *Our Lady and the Church*. Translated by Sebastian Bullock. New York: Pantheon, 1961.

Randers-Pehrson, Justine Davis. *Barbarians and Romans: The Birth Struggle of Europe, A.D. 400-700*. Norman: Oklahoma University Press, 1983.

Rawson, Elizabeth. "*Discrimina Ordinum: The Lex Julia Theatralis*." In *Roman Culture and Society: Collected Papers of Elizabeth Rawson*, 508-45. Oxford: Clarendon Press, 1991.

Rigby, Paul. "Original Sin." *ATAE* 607-15.

Rist, J. M. *The Road to Reality*. Cambridge: Cambridge University Press, 1967.

Rives, J. B. *Religion and Authority in Roman Carthage from Augustine to Constantine*. Oxford: Clarendon Press, 1995.

Rondet, Henri. *Original Sin: The Patristic and Theological Background*. Translated by C. Finegan. Staten Island: Alba House, 1972.

Ros, Karen E. "The Roman Theater at Carthage." Diss., University of Michigan, 1990.

Roussell, Aline. *Porneia: On Desire and the Body in Antiquity*. Translated by Felicia Pheasant. Oxford: Basil Blackwell, 1988.

Rush, Alfred C. *Death and Burial in Christian Antiquity*. SCA 1. Washington, DC: Catholic University of America Press, 1941.

Saller, Richard P. *Patriarchy, Property, and Death in the Roman Family*. Cambridge: Cambridge University Press, 1994.

Schoedel, William. *Ignatius of Antioch: A Commentary on the Letters of Saint Ignatius of Antioch*. Hermeneia. Philadelphia: Fortress Press, 1985.

Simonetti, Manlio. *La Produzione letteraria Latina fra Romani e Barbari (sec. V-Viil)*. Sussidi Patristici 3. Rome: Augustinianum, 1986.

———. "Studi sulla letteratura cristiana d'Africa in età vandalica." *Rencidonti del R. Istituto Lombardo de Scienze e Lettere* 83 (1950): 407-24.

————. "Theodore of Mopusestia." *EEC* 2824–25.

Soren, David, et al. *Carthage: From the Legends of the Aeneid to the Glorious Age of Gold.* New York: Simon & Schuster, 1991.

Steinhauser, K. *The Apocalypse Commentary of Tyconius: A History of Its Reception and Influence.* Frankfurt: Peter Lang, 1987.

TeSelle, Eugene. *Augustine the Theologian.* London: Burns and Oates, 1970.

Treggiari, Susan. "Ideals and Practicalities in Matchmaking in Ancient Rome." In *The Family in Antiquity to the Present,* edited by David I. Kertzer and Richard P. Saller, 91–108. New Haven: Yale University Press, 1991.

Van Slyke, Daniel G. "Quodvultdeus of Carthage: Political Change and Apocalyptic Theology in the Fifth-Century Roman Empire." Ph.D. diss., St. Louis University, 2001.

Wenger, A., ed. *Huit catéchèses baptismales inédites.* SC 50. Paris: Éditions du Cerf, 1957.

Wilken, Robert L. *John Chrysostom and the Jews: Rhetoric and Reality in the Late Fourth Century.* Berkeley: University of California Press, 1983.

————. *Judaism and the Early Christian Mind: A Study of Cyril of Alexandria's Exegesis and Theology.* New Haven: Yale University Press, 1971.

Wilkinson, John, ed. *Egeria's Travels.* Rev. 3rd ed. Warminster: Aris and Phillips, 1999.

SUBJECT INDEX

Adam, 57. *See also* "two Adams"

amphitheater, 15–16, 27–28. *See also* "spectacles"

apostolic succession, 55

apple (poison), 57. *See also* Satan

Arians (Homoian), 17–19, 28–34, 43–45, 49–50, 63–64, 79, 82

ascension, 78

audience of the creedal homilies, 8–10

Augustine of Hippo: the Arians, 18–19; catechumenate, 4–5; the Jews, 10–11; Quodvultdeus, 1–3, 19–20

Aurelius, Bishop, 2

baptism: Christ's death, 35–37; rebirth, 23, 67, 80; remission, 64

Berbers (also called Libyans or Tuaregs), 9, 13–14

burial of Christ, 59–61

Capriolus, Bishop, 3

Carthage, 9, 19. *See also* "spectacles"

catechesis, 4–5, 23, 67

catechumenate, 4–5

catechumens, 4–5

Christ: baptism of, 36; birth of, 72–72; Bridegroom, 35–36; Deliverer, 56; Eternal Salvation, 40; God-man, 73, 78; human and divine, 61–62; Judge, 62; Justice, 62; King, King of Kings, 69, 74, 80; Lamb, 37; Life, 81; Little One, 55, 56, 57; Living Bread, 48; Lord, 55; Man-Assumed, 32, 40, 62, 78; Mediator, 75; New Man, 59; Redeemer, 35; Risen One, 39; Savior, 55, 56, 57, 77; Shepherd, 79, 80; Son of Man, 31, 60; Sun of Justice, 48; True Life, 57

Chrysostom, John, 4

church: apostolic, 51; assembly of the faithful, 48; boundaries of, 81; bride, 36, 38, 48, 65, 81, 82; Church of God, 65–66; holy, 49, 57, 81; kingdom (as the), 48; mother, 23, 36–38, 49, 51, 57–58, 65, 67–68, 81, 82; perfect man, 48; sheep (as), 79–80; spiritual, 81

circus, 15–16